Lies Boys Believe

AND THE EPIC QUEST FOR TRUTH

Lies Boys Believe

AND THE EPIC QUEST FOR TRUTH

ERIN & JASON DAVIS

NANCY DeMOSS WOLGEMUTH LIES WE BELIEVE SERIES EDITOR

QUEST AHEAD

MOODY PUBLISHERS
CHICAGO

Unless otherwise indicated, all Scripture quotations are taken from the Holy Bible, New Living Translation, copyright © 1996, 2004, 2015 by Tyndale House Foundation. Used by permission of Tyndale House Publishers, Carol Stream, Illinois 60188. All rights reserved. Scripture quotations marked NLV are taken from the New Life Version, Copyright © 1969 and 2003. Used by permission of Barbour Publishing, Inc., Uhrichsville, Ohio 44683. All rights reserved. Scripture quotations marked (ESV) are from the ESV® Bible (The Holy Bible, English Standard Version®), copyright © 2001 by Crossway, a publishing ministry of Good News Publishers. Used by permission. All rights reserved. The ESV text may not be quoted in any publication made available to the public by a Creative Commons license. The ESV may not be translated in whole or in part into any other language. All emphasis in Scripture has been added.

Published in association with the literary agency of Wolgemuth & Wilson.

Edited by Amanda Cleary Eastep
Interior and cover design: Erik M. Peterson
Interior illustrations: Will Kelly
Cover camping themed illustrations copyright © 2023 by Artspace/Shutterstock (1090146080). All rights reserved. Cover illustrations of apple copyright © 2023 by Azure_Sun/Shutterstock (1721598025). All rights reserved. Cover illustrations of lined paper copyright © 2023 by Ann Precious/Shutterstock (108187301). All rights reserved. Dizzy face illustration copyright © 2023 by Le_Mon/Shutterstock (433530811). All rights reserved. Chapter opener illustrations copyright © 2023 by yodgin/Shutterstock (378323191). All rights reserved. Swiss army knife illustration copyright © 2023 by hchjjl/Shutterstock (303181334). All rights reserved. Figure 8 knot illustration copyright © 2023 by Maria Wong/Shutterstock (1137604631). All rights reserved. Seeds illustration copyright © 2023 by Valeriya Yanchkovskaya/Shutterstock (1993272521). All rights reserved. Armor of God illustrations copyright © 2023 by emilysk8/iStock (1428115075). All rights reserved. Author photo: Victoria Abel

Printed by: Bethany Press in Bloomington, MN – 08/2023

Library of Congress Cataloging-in-Publication Data

Names: Davis, Jason (Marketing manager), author. | Davis, Erin, 1980-
   author.
Title: Lies boys believe : and the epic quest for truth / Jason and Erin
   Davis.
Description: Chicago : Moody Publishers, [2023] | Includes bibliographical
   references. | Audience: Ages 8-12 | Summary: "Graphic novel meets meaty
   Bible teaching, helping boys identify ten core lies and replace them
   with Truth so they can stand firm. Your son will learn to swim against
   tides of deception and be equipped to recognize future lies as he
   develops a passion for knowing and living God's Word"-- Provided by
   publisher.
Identifiers: LCCN 2023007896 (print) | LCCN 2023007897 (ebook) | ISBN
   9780802429360 | ISBN 9780802473653 (ebook)
Subjects: LCSH: Boys--Religious life--Juvenile literature. | Christian
   life--Juvenile literature. | BISAC: JUVENILE NONFICTION / Religious /
   Christian / Values & Virtues | JUVENILE NONFICTION / Religious /
   Christian / Inspirational | LCGFT: Graphic novels
Classification: LCC BV4541.3 .D38 2023 (print) | LCC BV4541.3 (ebook) |
   DDC 248.832--dc23/eng/20230605
LC record available at https://lccn.loc.gov/2023007896
LC ebook record available at https://lccn.loc.gov/2023007897

Originally delivered by fleets of horse-drawn wagons, the affordable paperbacks from D. L. Moody's publishing house resourced the church and served everyday people. Now, after more than 125 years of publishing and ministry, Moody Publishers' mission remains the same—even if our delivery systems have changed a bit. For more information on other books (and resources) created from a biblical perspective, go to www.moodypublishers.com or write to:

Moody Publishers
820 N. LaSalle Boulevard
Chicago, IL 60610

1 3 5 7 9 10 8 6 4 2
Printed in the United States of America

To Eli, Noble, Judah, and Ezra

You are our greatest joy, our favorite people,
and our biggest blessing. May you stand firm against the
enemy's lies and hold high the banner of God's Truth.

Love always,

Dad & Mom

CONTENTS

MEET
YOUR GUIDES!

To read this page, turn your book to the right one quarter turn.

That was fun! Let's do it again. Turn your book clockwise one more quarter turn.

Are you dizzy?! We hope that's not the only time this book makes your head spin.

You are about to set out on an exciting adventure, a quest to discover the treasures buried in your Bible—God's Word. Any new and challenging expedition requires a guide. Good news! You've got **four guides** for this journey!

First, if you are a follower of Jesus, you've got **the Holy Spirit!** He is God Himself living inside of you (amazing, we know!). His job is to help you understand the Bible and obey it. He is always with you (Matthew 28:20), and He will never leave you or give up on you (Hebrews 13:5). Any time you come to something that is hard to understand in this book, stop and ask the Holy Spirit to give you wisdom. P.S. Being a follower of Jesus means more than just going to church or thinking Jesus was a great guy. John 3:16 tells us, "This is how God loved the world: He gave his one and only Son, so that everyone who believes in him will not perish but have eternal life." Do you believe in Jesus and that God loves you? Do you believe Jesus died so that you wouldn't have to perish in your sin? Have you asked Jesus to be the King of your life? If you're not sure, talk to an adult like a parent or a pastor at your church. This is the most important thing you can do in your life.

Second, you've got **godly grown-ups.** Whether it's your mom, dad, grandma, paw-paw, friend, or pastor, there is a big person in your life who loves you. (They probably bought you this book!) They may even be reading *A Parent's Guide to Lies Boys Believe* and learning right alongside you. Talk to them about what you're discovering and don't be afraid to ask them questions.

Finally, you have **us**, Jason and Erin Davis. **We are the parents of four wild and wonderful boys!** We wrote this book because we love them and because we love to see boys like *you* running away from lies and living out God's Truth!

If we could, we would have you over to our farm. You could pet a cow, chase a chicken, or pick a peach straight from our orchard. We might plan a hayride. We'd definitely roast some marshmallows! And we'd share how much God has done for us—and for you—so you'd be excited to experience knowing Him. This book is the next best thing.

This is a lie-busting, Truth-telling, fun-having book. Don't just read it! Work with it. Here are some ways to do that:

1. **Read it with your Bible close by. This book is important. God's book is more important!**
2. **As you read, fold down the top right corner of each odd-numbered page (it will look like a floppy dog ear). You'll discover an important message. This is a simple way you can build the habit of turning away from lies and embracing the Truth!**
3. **After you read each chapter, go back to the Contents page at the beginning of the book. Take a big, red marker and write over each lie, "Busted!" (Yes! We want you to write in this book!) This is another way you can express that you know God's Truth is worth standing on and you're not going to let lies have a hold on your life.**

The most important way to read this book is to **HAVE FUN!** Being a follower of Jesus is the most exciting adventure you'll ever be on. Enjoy it!

Let's roll,

Jason and Erin Davis

THE ADVENTURE BEGINS!

"Shotgun!"

Lenny and Thomas King yelled the word at the exact same nanosecond. Each boy glanced at the vehicle parked just a stone's throw away in their gravel driveway. Then they looked each other square in the eye and squinted—like two cowboys preparing for a showdown—each brother daring the other to make the first move. Then they took off running!

The finish line was the polished chrome handle on the passenger side of the van they'd be spending the next two weeks riding in. Lenny got there first, just a step ahead of his younger brother. The boys spun their arms and threw their elbows in a familiar struggle to pry the door open.

Lenny triumphed and hopped into the front passenger seat. He buckled himself in and stuck out his tongue at his brother.

"You rode shotgun last time," Thomas huffed.

"Fair is fair," Lenny replied, hitting the button to roll up the window.

Accepting his defeat, Thomas slid open the side door and climbed into the van. He flopped into the back seat behind his brother and crossed his arms over his chest.

From their seats in the van, the boys could see their parents standing close together on the front porch. Dad hugged Momma and their little brother and sister goodbye and slowly strolled toward them. Whistling a tune, he slid into the driver's seat and put on his aviator sunglasses.

"Ready for a big adventure?" he asked with a smile.

The brothers' frustration with each other disappeared. They were so excited, their bodies felt like they were filled with static electricity! Before they even left the driveway, Thomas was already daydreaming about his favorite road trip snacks: root beer, Skittles, and powdered sugar donuts. Lenny got busy loading the playlist he'd made. They were all imagining what two weeks of open road, nights around the campfire, and mountain trail hikes would be like.

Before Dad could put the van in gear, Momma slid open the van door. "You weren't going to leave without hugging your mom, were you?"

The boys wouldn't admit it in front of their friends, but their mom was one of their favorite people. She often shaped pancakes into their favorite comic book characters. She was always the loudest voice cheering from the stands at their sporting events. She invited them to snuggle in close each morning as she finished her cup of coffee and read the Bible, and she always found ways to show them how much they mattered to her.

"Can I pray for you?" Momma asked. Lenny had turned around in his seat to join Thomas and Momma in a group hug. It was a question they'd heard her ask often. It seemed like she was *always* praying for her kids.

"Lord, thank You for my sons," Momma prayed out loud. "Take care of them wherever they go. Help them to know that You're always with them. You will never leave them or forsake them. Help them become mighty men who tell the world about You. Amen."

"Amen," Dad echoed.

"Amen," Lenny and Thomas repeated.

They didn't always know how to show it, but the boys felt that growing up with parents who prayed for them every day and taught them to pray for each other was one of the best things about being a part of the King family.

"I'm going to miss you," Mom said. "But I hope you have the greatest adventure of your life!" Then she slid the van door closed again and walked back toward the house.

Dad blew a kiss to Mom before announcing, "Onward!"

Just a few days earlier, Lenny had blown out the twelve brightly colored birthday candles stuck into his mom's world-famous chocolate cake. After he'd eaten two huge helpings, he opened three presents wrapped in basketball-themed wrapping paper and discovered a bright orange sleeping bag from his parents and new leather hiking boots from his Nana and Pa. He also got the one thing he'd been begging for: his own phone. His birthday card read: "Pack your bags. You're going on an epic trip." A heart was drawn above "Mom and Dad." Lenny's younger brothers and sister had signed the card too: Thomas, Mikey (with the y backwards), and Lucy, whose name looked more like a scribble.

Sure, Lenny and Thomas fought sometimes about silly things (like who got to sit in the front seat), but they were best friends. Lenny was glad that Dad had agreed to let Thomas come. But where they were headed was a mystery. Dad had told them they were going to the mountains, but he'd kept the rest of the trip a secret, despite the boys' constant pestering. What they did know was that **this was going to be the adventure of a lifetime.**

. . .

As the van headed west and the hills of the Ozarks melted into the flat plains of Kansas, boredom set in. They'd already played the alphabet game (Thomas won) and spotted license plates from most of the fifty states minus Alaska, Hawaii, and Oregon (Dad was in the lead).

~~Alabama~~	~~Louisiana~~	~~Ohio~~
Alaska	~~Maine~~	~~Oklahoma~~
~~Arizona~~	~~Maryland~~	Oregon
~~Arkansas~~	~~Massachusetts~~	~~Pennsylvania~~
~~California~~	~~Michigan~~	~~Rhode Island~~
~~Colorado~~	~~Minnesota~~	~~South Carolina~~
~~Connecticut~~	~~Mississippi~~	~~South Dakota~~
~~Delaware~~	~~Missouri~~	~~Tennessee~~
~~Florida~~	~~Montana~~	~~Texas~~
~~Georgia~~	~~Nebraska~~	~~Utah~~
Hawaii	~~Nevada~~	~~Vermont~~
~~Idaho~~	~~New Hampshire~~	~~Virginia~~
~~Illinois~~	~~New Jersey~~	~~Washington~~
~~Indiana~~	~~New Mexico~~	~~West Virginia~~
~~Iowa~~	~~New York~~	~~Wisconsin~~
~~Kansas~~	~~North Carolina~~	~~Wyoming~~
~~Kentucky~~	~~North Dakota~~	

**Circle all the states you've been to on the list above.
Put a star beside the three states you most want to visit.**

"I've got an idea," Thomas said. "Let's play two truths and a lie."

It was a game his Sunday school teacher sometimes played to wake up their brains.

"The rules are simple," he explained. "You tell us two truths and one lie, and we try to guess the lie."

"I'll go first," Dad volunteered.

"This is going to be easy!" Lenny blurted. "We've known you our *whole lives.*"

Thomas agreed, but didn't say anything. He was usually quieter than his older brother, plus sometimes Dad surprised him.

"I wanted to be an architect when I was your age," Dad said first.

"That's the lie," Lenny yelled before his dad even finished his sentence.

Mr. King was a pastor. He loved leading their small country church. And although Thomas hadn't said anything yet, he agreed with Lenny. He couldn't imagine his dad ever wanting to do any other job.

Dad looked into the rearview mirror and winked. "When I was sixteen, I drove by myself to the same mountains we're going to. I spent two weeks biking and sleeping under the stars."

"*That's* got to be the lie," Thomas said. "I know Nana. She doesn't let us out of her sight when we're at her house. There's no way she would let you go on a trip by yourself!"

Plus, Thomas thought, *I have never seen you ride a mountain bike.*

Dad laughed out loud. *Did that mean he was telling the truth or a lie?* both boys wondered.

"My shoe size is 14," Dad added.

Now they were really stumped.

"You do have big feet," Lenny said.

Thomas's forehead wrinkled as he tried to picture the hiking boots that were lined up next to the suitcases behind him. *Sure, Dad's feet were bigger than his*, he thought, *but were they that much bigger?*

"It's got to be the architect," Lenny said confidently.

"I can't imagine Nana letting you take a trip like this one," Thomas repeated. "That's the lie."

"Wrong and wrong again," Dad said with a laugh. "My shoes are size 12."

"You wanted to be an architect?" both boys said at once, their eyes wide with surprise.

The miles passed more quickly as Dad told stories about when he was a teenager and how God had called him to go to Bible college, become a pastor, and "build" a church instead of building skyscrapers. Before they knew it, the sun started to sink below the horizon and the whole sky lit up with bright colors of orange, red, and pink.

A brown sign with a yellow tent symbol pointed the way to the campground. Dad took the exit off the interstate and soon pulled the van into an area with lots of trees.

Once their blue tent was up and their sleeping bags were rolled out side by side, the boys gathered sticks and Dad built a campfire.

They roasted hot dogs for dinner and made s'mores with marshmallows and peanut butter cups. As they sat in silence staring at the red, orange, and blue flames, Dad pulled out his favorite book, the Bible, and opened it close to the beginning. Lenny and Thomas got comfortable in their camp chairs as frogs sang loudly from the trees that surrounded them. The fire crackled and popped and sent a trail of sparks and smoke swirling upward. They could see the orange glow of other fires and the silhouettes of families camping nearby. Flashlights flickered on and off, and children squealed in the distance as some played capture the flag and hide-and-seek. Thomas's fingers were sticky from his s'more, and he tried to wipe the gooey mess on his pants without being noticed.

How do you like your marshmallow cooked? **Circle your answer below.**

I don't know. I've never cooked a marshmallow.

Golden brown

Warm and gooey all the way through

Burnt and black

On fire!

The boys were used to seeing their dad with his Bible open. He read it to them and their younger siblings most evenings before bed. He held it as he preached the sermon every Sunday morning at church. Sometimes, they could tell their dad was feeling stressed because he paced the long hallway in their house with his Bible open and his lips moving in prayer.

Their mom loved the Scriptures too. Each morning they'd mosey downstairs as the smell of fresh coffee wafted up to their bedrooms. They'd almost always find her curled up on the couch with her Bible open on her lap, still wearing her faded yellow bathrobe and fuzzy slippers.

Like all parents, Mom wasn't perfect. Sometimes a switch seemed to flip as she shifted from quietly reading her Bible to becoming a four-star general, barking out orders for the kids to get ready for school.

Still, she filled page after page in her journal with notes about what she learned as she read God's Word.

"What do you write in there?" Thomas asked once as he watched her scribbling away.

"Questions . . . prayers . . . things I notice . . . more questions," she replied. "The Bible is God's love letter to me. I like to write love letters back to Him."

Thomas liked that idea. He had begun writing in the margins of his Bible too at times. He wasn't sure he was doing it right, but Momma told him there wasn't a wrong way to learn God's Word.

"This is my happy place," she would tell her kids as she pulled them in close and read the Bible out loud. Often, they didn't understand what she read. The names sounded funny, and the rules didn't always make sense, but they knew that reading the Bible always put a smile on their mom's face.

Most nights she tucked the King kids in with a Bible story. Like the familiar rhythm of the sun rising and setting, their mom began and ended most days with her Bible open and her eyes closed in prayer.

. . .

Dad clicked on his army green headlamp. Steam rose from the coffee in his stainless-steel camp mug, wrapping his face in an eerie glow. "This is more than just a birthday trip," he said. "I want you to think of it as a hunt for treasure."

Lenny imagined piles of pirate treasure stashed into hidden lairs. Thomas pictured stacks of gold bars.

As if he could read their minds, Dad said, "It might not be the treasure you're thinking of." He paused. "I promise, it's even better!"

A real-life treasure hunt! Thomas bounced up and down as if he was suddenly filled with helium, though his pants were stuck to his chair with marshmallow goo. He'd never been this excited!

"But first," Dad continued, "we need to know who the bad guy is. Let me read you Genesis 3."

"There are villains in the Bible?" Thomas asked as he licked gooey chocolate that had oozed between his fingers.

"Yeah, and this one is the scaly kind," Dad explained. "One day a serpent slithered into the perfect garden God had made for the first man and woman . . .

"Let me show you," he said, and he began to read:

> One day he asked the woman, "Did God really say you must not eat the fruit from any of the trees in the garden?"
>
> "Of course we may eat fruit from the trees in the garden," the woman replied. "It's only the fruit from the tree in the middle of the garden that we are not allowed to eat. God said, 'You must not eat it or even touch it; if you do, you will die.'" (Genesis 3:1–3)

As the darkness settled in for the night, the hot summer air started to cool. Crickets joined the symphony with the frogs. Thomas didn't say it, but he felt a little homesick. He missed his mom, his dog, and his favorite fuzzy blanket, but wasn't sure if he dared to tell his brother.

"Hey, we learned about this last week in Sunday school," Lenny blurted out, interrupting Thomas's train of thought. "I don't think that's exactly what God said about the tree."

"Good catch," Dad replied. "And you're right. God told Adam he could eat all the fruit he wanted from any tree in the garden *except* the tree of the knowledge of good and evil. He did warn Adam that if he ate the fruit from the wrong tree, he would die. God didn't say anything about touching it."

"So, Satan's words were more like an exaggeration?" Thomas asked. "Exaggerating isn't really lying, is it, Dad?"

"Well, is exaggerating the same thing as telling the absolute truth?" Dad asked.

"I guess not," Thomas said.

"The serpent was lying when he said that God wouldn't let them eat from any of the trees in the garden, and Eve was lying when she exaggerated what God said," Dad explained. "Let's keep reading . . ."

> "You won't die!" the serpent replied to the woman. "God knows that your eyes will be opened as soon as you eat it, and you will be like God, knowing both good and evil." (Genesis 3:4–5)

Both boys stared at their dad, waiting for him to say more. Instead, he closed his Bible and yawned like he was ready for bed.

"What does that old Bible story have to do with finding treasure?" Lenny asked.

Dad finished the last of his campfire coffee. He smiled as he rinsed out his metal mug. "I can't reveal all the mysteries on the first day. It's time to get some sleep. We hit the road early tomorrow morning."

Tag, You're It!

Look up Genesis 2:16–17 and Genesis 3:1 in your Bible. Hint: Genesis is the first book of the Bible. Two truths and a lie about what God said are listed below. Circle the lie:

1. God told Adam he could eat from all the trees in the garden except one special tree.

2. God told Adam and Eve they couldn't eat from *any* of the trees in the garden.

3. God told Adam that if he ate from the tree of the knowledge of good and evil, he would die.

The villain in this story is the devil, also known as Satan. He's the villain in your story too. Listen to how the Bible describes him in John 8:44:

> He was a murderer from the beginning. He has always hated the truth, because there is no truth in him. When he lies, it is consistent with his character; for he is a liar and the father of lies.

To understand why this matters, you need to know what lies are and what Truth is.

LIE (verb)
To make an untrue statement
with intent to deceive.[1]

TRUTH (noun)
The real facts about something:
the things that are true.[2]

Pretty simple, right? Truth is true and a lie . . . isn't? But it's not always easy to tell the difference. Just as he did with Adam and Eve in the garden of Eden, the devil *will* lie to you. So, how can you know if something is true? Read what Jesus said in John 17:17: Your word is truth." (ESV)

The Bible is God's Word, which makes it more than a book. It's like a treasure map, written by God to help us discover what's true and what isn't.

1. *Merriam-Webster*, s.v. "lie (v.)," https://www.merriam-webster.com/dictionary/lie.
2. *Merriam-Webster*, s.v. "truth (n.)," https://www.merriam-webster.com/dictionary/truth.

. . .

Lenny and Thomas lay wide awake listening to the chirping of crickets and tree frogs all around them. Thomas kept shining his flashlight under his chin and making funny faces to get his brother to laugh. They tried to whisper so they didn't wake their dad up, though there wasn't much chance of that. He probably couldn't hear *anything* above the sound of his own snoring. Eventually both boys drifted off to sleep with visions of treasure floating into their dreams.

LIE #1:
"Reading the Bible just isn't for me."
TRUTH:
The Bible is your treasure!

*N*ote: This chapter is a little longer than the others, but don't let that spook you. It's interactive! Have you ever imagined what it's like to go inside a dark mine? Or solved a cryptogram? Grab your favorite snack and settle in. You're about to join the adventure!

. . .

"Wake up, sleepyhead," Dad said, as he gently kicked the bottom of Lenny's foot.

Lenny hadn't moved a muscle all morning.

The sun was already rising, and everything was beginning to bake in the sizzling summer heat. Dad and Thomas had already cooked scrambled eggs over the fire, before rinsing out their dishes and loading most of their supplies back into the van.

Thomas had always been an early riser. Lenny . . . not so much.

Lenny groaned and rolled over. His blond hair was already starting to stick to his sweaty forehead. "Five more minutes!" he mumbled from inside that hazy state between wakefulness and sleep. He heard the sounds of his dad and brother around him but kept drifting back into his dreams.

"We've got to get moving, bud," Dad replied. "Help us pack up the tent. Adventure awaits!"

The boys had a lot of practice working together. Lenny usually took the lead. His parents and teachers often told him that he was a good leader. He just seemed to know how to get the job done. Taking the tent down and breaking down the long tent poles was the easy part. Getting everything back into the nylon tent bag required teamwork, but with some patience and creativity, the boys managed to do it without Dad's help. Before long they were back in the van with miles of open road ahead of them.

When lunchtime hit, the travelers devoured greasy cheeseburgers and thick chocolate milkshakes from a diner in the first town they came to. Dad insisted that they eat in the car instead of going in. "We have to be somewhere before sundown," he said mysteriously.

Late in the afternoon, they pulled down a long, dusty driveway that led to a small log cabin. Brown chickens pecked the ground in the front yard. On the big front porch of the cabin,

a man with a long white beard and faded overalls tilted back and forth on a wooden rocker. Next to him, an old red dog was snoozing in the summer heat.

"Who's that?" Thomas whispered.

"That's Pastor Ralph," Dad replied.

Ralph had led the church Dad attended growing up. Through the years, the boys had heard stories about the pastor who had encouraged Dad to read the Bible every day. It was something he had done since he was just eight years old.

"You didn't tell us your pastor was so . . . old," Lenny said.

"Or that he lived with so many chickens!"
Thomas added.

Dad laughed. "Well, he wasn't old when he
was my pastor," he said. "We've both
changed a lot since then. After
Pastor Ralph retired and his wife
died, he moved
here to be closer
to his grandkids.

"Building his own
cabin had always been
a dream of his. He built this whole place with his own two
hands," Dad added proudly.

"Cool!" Thomas said, as he began studying the cabin's
architecture. He loved to look at blueprints and think about
how things are built. He often built cabins and lean-tos with
sticks and branches in the yard, and he and his brothers would
pretend they were pioneers or gold miners or sailors marooned
on a deserted island. He knew enough about building to
recognize that Pastor Ralph's cabin was built by a true
craftsman.

Dad pulled the van under the shade of a big elm tree. Everyone
climbed out and stretched and yawned. The long hours in the
car without much to look at had made them sleepy.

"Welcome, adventurers!" Pastor Ralph boomed. He walked slowly down the porch steps, his dog matching his stride. As he reached the van, he threw out his hand for a shake. He shook each boy's hand enthusiastically before giving their dad a big bear hug. "I remember when you were their size," he said.

"That seems like a long time ago," Dad said.

"How's that wife of yours?" Ralph asked.

"As beautiful, kind, and smart as ever," Dad said, beaming.

Dad was always saying mushy stuff like that about Mom. Though the boys often rolled their eyes and sometimes pretended like they were gagging over the things their parents said about each other, secretly, they liked it.

"Are you hungry?" Ralph asked.

Even though they'd each gulped down a double cheeseburger, fries, and a shake for lunch, both boys yelled "Yes!" at the exact same time.

"Pinch, poke, you owe me a coke," Thomas said a split second before his brother did.

Dad put his arm around Ralph. "Growing boys are *always* hungry."

"Cookies and milk are waiting for you on the table," Pastor Ralph announced. "But eat them quickly. You've got a puzzle to solve."

A *puzzle?* Thomas imagined a 1,000-piece jigsaw puzzle. Lenny was picturing a crossword. But they didn't stop to ask questions. Those cookies were calling their names.

Inside the cabin, each boy stuffed a cookie in his mouth and gulped down a tall glass of cold milk.

"These boys act like they haven't eaten in weeks," Ralph teased. "Grab those lanterns," he added, nodding toward the corner of the kitchen.

Two old-fashioned oil lanterns sat on the floor. The metal looked like it had been painted red at some point, but the color had faded to a pinkish orange. Small patches of rust dotted each one. The glass domes were streaked with black soot from years of use. They matched the look of Pastor Ralph's cabin perfectly: functional but not exactly stylish. Everything that hung on the log walls looked like it was from another era, including deer antlers, old snow shoes, and faded pictures of Pastor Ralph's family.

Each boy grabbed a lantern and followed Pastor Ralph out the back door. His yard was littered with old items that most would consider junk. Wooden wheels, rusty farm equipment, and trucks and mowers in various states of repair rose from the crabgrass in every direction. Several projects, obviously assembled from spare parts, included a homemade wind chime dangling from a tree and rusty hubcaps shaped into a sculpture on the shed wall.

Lenny was itching to dig through the piles to see what he could find, but he stuck with the group.

Pastor Ralph led them to a dark opening in the side of the hill that gaped like the mouth of a monster.

"This is an old mine," Dad explained. "Long before Pastor Ralph bought this land, men used to go in through this opening every day and come out with carts of coal."

"Cool!" Lenny exclaimed.

"Creepy," Thomas said more quietly.

"You're going in . . . without us," Dad announced. "But you're not looking for coal. You're looking for *treasure*."

Their eyes got wide with excitement.

"In fact," Dad continued, "you're looking for one of the greatest treasures a person can ever find."

Pastor Ralph pulled a box of matches from the front pocket of his overalls. He struck one on the rock opening and lit each

boy's lantern. Then he blew out the match before showing them how to carry the lanterns so the flame wouldn't go out.

"You're on your own from here. You'll know what you're looking for when you find it."

Lenny was off and running into the mine before Pastor Ralph had even finished his sentence.

Thomas hung back, feeling a little unsure. "Is it safe, Dad?"

"Well, all treasure hunts have some risk, I suppose," Dad replied, putting his hands on Thomas's shoulders. "But stick with your brother. You have your lamp, and Pastor Ralph and I will stay right here. If you get scared, just come back toward the light."

Hesitantly at first, Thomas followed his brother into the mine. "Lenny, wait up!" His words seemed to bounce off the walls.

"Lenny!"
  "Lenny . . ."
  "Lenny . . ."

"Wait up!"
  "Wait up . . ."
  "Wait up . . ."

The tunnel was filled with old wood mining carts and some broken tools. They heard the sound of wings flapping overhead before they saw the silhouettes of bats diving back and forth between the shaft walls. The air smelled musty, like the patch of dirt under their front porch where they would sometimes dig for fishing worms after it rained. The underground world was mostly quiet . . . and dark. Soon, the boys couldn't see much beyond what was in the small circles of light provided by their lanterns. The light coming from the mine opening behind them was growing dimmer when Thomas suddenly bumped into something.

"Ouch!" he said. "What was that?"

Both boys held their lanterns above their heads, expanding the ring of light.

"It's a table," Thomas said. "Looks like there's a note."

Sitting on a small table was an old wooden box. On top of the box was a note from Pastor Ralph.

Dear Lenny and Thomas,

There is a treasure worth more than silver or gold inside this box. If you can open it, the treasure is yours to keep forever. But you have to break the code first.

Best,
Pastor Ralph

A	B	C	D	E	F	G	H	I	J	K	L	M
				15				13				

N	O	P	Q	R	S	T	U	V	W	X	Y	Z
20				4	14	16						

F _ R S T _ S _ _ F T
15 26 3 4   14 16 25 24 14   21 25 15 16

T _ _ N _ _ _ S T _ S
16 7 25 20   16 22 26   14 16 25 24 14

R I _ _ T _ T _ _ _ _ _
4 13 23 7 16   16 7 25   18 25 2   2 26 3

S _ _ _ I S _ I _ I N
14 25 25 18   13 14   7 13 8 13 20 23

I N _ _ _ _ _ I N S I _ T
13 20   24 21 11 13 20   14 13 23 7 16

Underneath Pastor Ralph's signature, there were a bunch of letters and numbers that didn't make any sense.

"What could the treasure be?" Thomas asked.

"What's worth more than silver or gold?" Lenny wondered out loud.

"A million dollars!" Thomas said.

"Or a key to a new sports car," Lenny responded. "Let's find out!"

Thomas set the note on the table, picked up the box, and felt along the edges. It was sealed shut. He tried to use his lantern to see the box in detail, but it was tough to hold the box and his lantern, so he set it down on the cool dirt floor.

"I can't see!" Thomas said to his brother. "Hold your lantern closer."

"On it!" Lenny said as he held his lantern right in front of the box. "There's a lock!" he exclaimed.

On the front of the box, a brass plate surrounding a small keyhole gleamed in the lantern light. But where was the key?

Thomas set the box back on top of the table. Lenny held his lantern high as his brother felt around and under the table. No key. Lenny dropped the lantern lower as his brother got down on his hands and knees and felt the ground. Nothing. Thomas picked up the note again. "This must be the puzzle Pastor Ralph was talking about," he reasoned.

Lenny could almost see an imaginary light bulb turn on above his head.

"I know what those letters mean!" Thomas blurted. "It's a cryptogram."

"A cryptowhat?" Lenny asked.

"A cryptogram. I love these. It's like a word puzzle."

The boys hunched over the table, shoulder to shoulder, as they studied Pastor Ralph's note more closely.

Tag, You're It!

Try to solve the cryptogram on the next page. It's the same one Lenny and Thomas discovered in the mine. Each letter has a corresponding number. We've given you a few letters to get you started. For example, F = 15. Think about words and patterns you know, like how an "in" at the end of the word is usually followed by a "g," as in fish*ing*. Once you figure out the letter in one spot, fill it in for all the spots with the same number.

A	B	C	D	E	F	G	H	I	J	K	L	M
				15				13				

N	O	P	Q	R	S	T	U	V	W	X	Y	Z
20				4	14	16						

F _ R _   S T _ _ _   S _ _ FT
15 26 3 4   14 16 25 24 14   21 25 15 16

T _ _ _   N _ _   S T _ _ _
16 7 25 20   16 22 26   14 16 25 24 14

R I _ _ _   T _ _   T _ _   _ _ _
4 13 23 7 16   16 7 25   18 25 2   2 26 3

S _ _ _   I S   I _ _ I N
14 25 25 18   13 14   7 13 8 13 20 23

I N   _ _ _ I N   S I _ _ T
13 20   24 21 11 13 20   14 13 23 7 16

43

Thomas scratched his head.

Lenny looked at the puzzle for less than a minute. "This is impossible!" he shouted.

"Just give me a minute," Thomas whispered. "I can do this."

In the dim light, Lenny watched as a serious expression moved across his brother's face. He'd seen that look before. Thomas had a knack for figuring out riddles and math problems that others couldn't.

"Start with the short words . . . look for patterns," Thomas said, though Lenny could tell his brother was mostly talking to himself. Seconds later he shouted, "I've got the first word!" His voice echoed from the mine walls. "It's four!"

"Four what?" Lenny asked.

"I don't know yet," his brother said.

Thomas picked his lantern up off the mine floor and placed it on the table. The seconds ticked away while he worked on the puzzle.

Lenny explored the mine as he waited, but he didn't venture too far from his brother. He wanted his share of the treasure too. (Plus, he was a little more scared than he let on.) As he wandered along the shaft walls, he stubbed his toe on something sticking up from the dirt.

"Ouch!" Lenny yelled before reaching down to see what he'd hit. It was an old pickax, probably left behind by a miner after a long day of work. He picked it up and examined the metal head, rusted by time. Lenny headed back toward his brother, who was still hunched over the table with a look of concentration on his face. Just as Lenny was about to suggest they could pry the box open with the pickax, Thomas exclaimed, "I've got it!"

"Well . . . what does it say?"

A	B	C	D	E	F	G	H	I	J	K	L	M
11	17	6	8	25	15	23	7	13	9	18	21	5

N	O	P	Q	R	S	T	U	V	W	X	Y	Z
20	26	24	12	4	14	16	3	19	22	10	2	1

F O U R   S T E P S   L E F T
15 26 3 4   14 16 25 24 14   21 25 15 16

T H E N   T W O   S T E P S
16 7 25 20   16 22 26   14 16 25 24 14

R I G H T   T H E   K E Y   Y O U
4 13 23 7 16   16 7 25   18 25 2   2 26 3

S E E K   I S   H I D I N G
14 25 25 18   13 14   7 13 8 13 20 23

I N   P L A I N   S I G H T
13 20   24 21 11 13 20   14 13 23 7 16

45

"Four steps left, then two steps right," Thomas read. "The key you seek is hiding in plain sight."

"I'm sure glad we brought your big brain on this trip," Lenny said, giving his brother a high five. "Let me see."

Lanterns in hand, they turned away from the box so they were facing the mine wall on the left. They took four steps.

"Then two steps right," Thomas repeated, and they both stepped right.

"Yikes! A bat hit me," Lenny yelled, wiping his forehead after running into something cold and solid.

"What did it feel like?" Thomas asked.

"Like I got hit with something metal."

Immediately they both held their lanterns above their heads. Thomas saw it first. Lenny was busy swatting at whatever he imagined had attacked him.

"That's not a bat!" Thomas said. "It's a key!!"

Sure enough, dangling from a long string attached to the mine ceiling was a small brass key. How had they missed it before? In a space filled with items from the past, the bright shiny key looked obviously out of place. A few bats hung from the ceiling near the string where the key was attached.

"You found it!" Lenny said before high-fiving his brother again.

Thomas had a collection of old keys in a big glass jar back home. This looked like one of his skeleton keys. It was made of heavy brass. On the top was an ornate design of swirls and loops, attached to a shaft that was about two and a half inches long with a small plate on the bottom. Thomas handed his lantern to Lenny and untied the key. They hurried back to the box, and Thomas shoved the key into the lock.

"Are you ready to get rich?" Thomas asked his brother.

"You know it," Lenny replied.

"One, two, three . . ." Thomas let the excitement build before turning the key in the lock. The hinges squeaked as he pried the lid open to reveal two books stacked one on top of the other. Thomas took each one out of the box. One had Lenny King embossed in gold leaf on the cover. The other said Thomas King in silver letters.

"Books?" Lenny asked, clearly disappointed. "How can books be worth more than silver or gold?"

"These aren't just any books," Thomas said. "These are Bibles. Looks like there is one for each of us." He was disappointed too, but he tried not to show it.

"Maybe these are just clues for another puzzle," Lenny said. "Let's go ask Dad."

They emerged from the mine carrying their lanterns and new Bibles. Dad and Pastor Ralph sat beside a fire that glowed inside a ring of smooth stones. The air smelled of smoke and bug spray. Pastor Ralph was reading a Bible passage the boys knew their dad had heard a zillion times. Still, Dad was so interested in what his old friend was saying he didn't even notice Lenny and Thomas until they walked up to the campfire.

"Well, did you find any treasure?" Pastor Ralph asked. He closed his Bible before setting it down on the grass. He started rubbing his hands together above the campfire.

"We found a couple of Bibles, if that's what you mean," Thomas replied, passing his Bible to his dad. He'd already set his lantern down near the mine entrance, and he hoped no one noticed his disappointment.

Ralph kept his eyes on the flames as he said, "Did you know that one of the people who wrote the Bible said, 'Your instructions are more valuable to me than millions in gold and silver'?"

"So . . . the Bibles *are* the treasure?" Lenny asked.

"I'm not sure it's worth millions," Thomas added quietly, kicking at some small rocks with the toe of his boot. His dad passed the Bible back, and Thomas ran his fingers along his name embossed on the cover.

Pastor Ralph laughed. "I thought you might say that," he said. "And I understand. I was about your age when my dad sat me down and encouraged me to start reading the Bible every day. It felt like he was giving me extra schoolwork, but because I loved my dad and I knew he loved me, I did it. It was hard at first, but it didn't take long before I started to enjoy the time I spent reading the Bible. Over the years, the Bible has become one of my greatest treasures."

"That's part of the reason I wanted to take this trip with you boys," Dad added. "You're growing up, and I don't just want your bodies to grow bigger and stronger, I want you to grow bigger and stronger in your friendship with Jesus. The Bible is a gift God has given you to help you grow."

"Are you telling us we *have* to read the Bible every day?" Thomas asked as he sat down next to Pastor Ralph. His brother plopped down in a camp chair nearby.

"No," Dad replied. "No one can make you love the Bible, but watching Pastor Ralph's love for the Bible when I was a boy made me want to read it, and my hope is that as you grow up and watch your mom and me love the Bible, you'll love it too . . . that it will become your treasure."

"I try to read it," Lenny explained. He picked up a small stick and started poking at the coals in the fire ring. His Bible sat unopened on his lap. "But sometimes it feels boring. Other times it doesn't make much sense to me, or I can't figure out how what I am reading applies to my life. I dunno, Dad. Maybe the Bible just isn't for me."

"Can I tell you a secret?" Pastor Ralph asked, as he poked at some glowing embers with a stick.

"Sure," Lenny replied.

"I don't always understand the Bible either, and I was a pastor for a looong time. I don't always feel like reading it. Sometimes I'd rather be fishing, but when that happens I ask God to help me want to read and to help me search after the Truth found in the Bible . . ."

"The same way I would search for silver and gold?" Lenny asked.

"You got it!" Pastor Ralph replied.

"The Bible is one of God's greatest gifts to us," Dad interjected. "It's more than a book. It shows us who God is, and it teaches us how God wants us to live."

"Is that why you and Momma read it so much?" Thomas asked.

"Yep," Dad replied. "While you two were in the mine, Pastor Ralph and I were talking about Proverbs 2:1–5. He taught me to love these verses when I was a kid like you."

"What's it about?" Thomas asked, genuinely curious. He knew the book of Proverbs was in the Old Testament. He worked to try and find it in his new Bible as mosquitoes buzzed around his head.

"Mind if I read it to you?" Pastor Ralph replied. His old, worn Bible was already open on his lap.

"Sure," Thomas said. He still wasn't convinced the Bible could be as interesting as his comic books or the adventure novels he and his brother liked to swap back and forth.

"Here it goes," Pastor Ralph said.

"My child, listen to what I say,
    and treasure my commands.

Tune your ears to wisdom,
    and concentrate on understanding.

Cry out for insight,
and ask for understanding."

A serious look came across his face as he read the next verse.
He looked into the eyes of each boy and then their dad.

"Search for them as you would for silver;
seek them like hidden treasures.

Then you will understand what it means to fear the LORD,
and you will gain knowledge of God."

The four of them sat in silence, staring at the smoke rising in
a long column from the fire. Lenny had gone to church nearly
every Sunday of his life, only missing when he was sick and
Momma stayed home to take care of him. He had tried to
read the Bible on his own many times before, but it never held
his attention for long. But seeing how reading the Bible made
his dad and Pastor Ralph light up, he suddenly found himself
wanting to love the Bible like they did. There was something
about the way their voices got when they read it that made him
feel . . . inspired.

Thomas's mind was spinning too. He hated disappointing
people, especially his dad, but he couldn't help thinking that
the Bible just wasn't for him. He loved to read. That wasn't
the problem. He often hid under his covers and read books by
flashlight long after his parents kissed him goodnight. But he

just didn't see what a book written so long ago had anything to do with his life.

Their dad broke the silence.

"Lenny, do you remember what your birthday card said?" he asked.

After thinking for a moment, Lenny replied, "Something about an epic adventure?"

"That's right. The real quest begins now. I'm not just talking about the adventures we're going to have on this trip, although I hope we have some epic ones. I'm talking about the search to know God through His Word."

"You want us to see our Bibles as treasure?" Lenny asked, holding his up in the air.

The boys could tell this meant a lot to their dad. He was the best person they knew and they both wanted to grow up to be just like him. They still had a lot of questions, but they were ready to learn more. Maybe the Bible was more than just a big old book after all.

"Ready for your next quest?" Pastor Ralph asked.

"Will there be bats involved?" Thomas asked as he used his hands to make a flapping noise over his brother's head.

"No bats," Pastor Ralph laughed. "I want you to read your Bible every day for the rest of your trip. Start in the book of John. It's a bunch of stories about what Jesus did when He lived on earth. When you get home, talk to your dad about whether or not you still feel like the Bible isn't for you. Deal?"

"Deal," Lenny said.

"Deal," his brother repeated.

"Let's shake on it," Pastor Ralph added.

The boys gave him a firm handshake, just like their dad had taught them to.

"I think there's some cookies left in the kitchen," Pastor Ralph said, changing the subject.

"Last one there's a rotten egg!" Lenny yelled.

Hours later, with their bellies full of cookies, the boys climbed into the bunk beds in Pastor Ralph's guest room and soon drifted off to sleep. Their new Bibles sat nearby, full of treasure and waiting to be opened.

Tag, You're It!

Look up Psalm 119:65–72 in your Bible. **Circle these words:**

Commands

Word

Decrees

Commandments

Instructions

Though there are many different words used in this psalm, they all describe God's Word. A psalm is really a song, and although the author isn't named, some believe it may have been written by King David. He was a giant-slaying, sword-fighting, battle-winning king. He loved adventure as much as you do. Even though he was a rich king, God's Word was his greatest treasure. He wrote:

"Your laws are my treasure; they are my heart's delight" (Psalm 119:111).

And . . .

"I rejoice in your word like one who discovers a great treasure" (Psalm 119:162).

And . . .

"Your instructions are more valuable to me than millions in gold and silver" (Psalm 119:72).

What makes the Bible so valuable? The apostle Paul tells us in Ephesians 6:17, "Take the sword of the Spirit, which is the word of God."

Imagine if the boys had found a silver sword that helped them win their battles against the fiercest enemy hiding out inside that old mine. What a wonderful treasure that would be! God's Word works like a different kind of sword, helping you fight back against Satan's lies so you can win the battle and stand firm on God's Truth.

God's Word = Your Treasure

Have you ever believed the lie that the Bible just isn't for you? The villain, the devil, knows what a treasure the Bible is, and he knows that it's full of wisdom that will help you know who God is. He spreads lies like:

- The Bible is just an ordinary book.
- The Bible isn't true.
- The Bible is boring.
- The Bible isn't for you.

But you know the Truth. The Bible is God's Word! It is one of the greatest treasures God gives His kids.

You've already learned a lot about the Bible.

- The Bible is a treasure map that helps you discover God's Truth.
- The Bible is a sword that helps you fight against the lies of the enemy.
- The Bible is a treasure, worth more than silver or gold.

But that doesn't mean you will always feel like reading it. **Feelings aren't facts.** Sometimes you will want to read the Bible and sometimes . . . you just . . won't. (Do you *always* feel like brushing your teeth, making your bed, or being nice to your siblings?) God has a lot to show you in His Word. It takes practice and the help of parents, teachers, and friends to better understand what God wants you to know. But instead of thinking about it like a homework assignment, think of it like a treasure hunt. There's gold in them thar hills!

Take the 30-Day Challenge

You'll never love the Bible less by reading it more. In fact, the opposite will happen. The more you read it, the more you will treasure it!

So, as you continue your journey along with Lenny and Thomas, join them in taking Pastor Ralph's challenge. Read your Bible every day for the next thirty days. Start in the book of John. (You will find a 30-day journey through the book of John in the back of this book.) Then take some time to talk to someone in your family about what you're learning. **If you're up to the challenge, sign your name on the line below.**

I'm Ready to Take the 30-Day Bible Reading Challenge!

Signed:

_____

LIE #2:
"I'm good enough."

TRUTH:
You need Jesus.

They stayed at Pastor Ralph's for a few more days. He showed them his favorite fishing hole, and they caught so many large-mouthed bass and sunny-bellied perch that their stringers were full. Pastor Ralph grilled their catch, made homemade fries and hush puppies for dinner, and let them drink as much soda as they wanted.

Pastor Ralph taught Lenny how to whittle. They sat together for hours carving thick branches into small spoons.

Thomas liked exploring the area around the cabin looking for rocks. He found some with white and pink crystals spiking in every direction. Others looked like they were made of glass. He even found some shiny fool's gold the color of Momma's wedding band that glinted in the summer sun. He lined his finds up along the back bumper of the van like a collection in a museum.

At night they'd circle up around the campfire and talk about lots of things: sports, movies, fishing . . . but Pastor Ralph often brought the conversation back to Jesus and the Bible. It was obvious to both boys that his faith was the most important thing to him. Other than their dad, they'd never met anyone who loved Jesus so much and was also strong, fun, and easy to be around.

"Pastor Ralph, I want to be just like you when I grow up," Lenny said as the two sat together working on their spoons.

"Thank you," Pastor Ralph replied, "that makes my heart happy." He smiled at Lenny as wood shavings flipped from the stick he was carving. He set it aside and reached down to pat his old dog, who was napping at their feet.

Then, one morning Dad announced it was time to hit the road again. Lenny was a little sad. Pastor Ralph treated him like a man, not a kid: trusting him to handle a pocketknife, clean fish, and build the campfire on his own. He wasn't ready to leave. Thomas, on the other hand, had explored every corner of the property. He was eager to discover something new. Pastor Ralph let him keep an old bucket he found in an abandoned shed to put his rocks in so he could add them to his collection back home.

"Remember that the Bible is a treasure," Pastor Ralph said as they were loading up the van.

"I'll remember," Lenny said.

"I'll remember too," Thomas added. "And if you ever find any *real* treasure in that mine, you've got to share it with us."

"The Bible *is* real," Pastor Ralph said with a laugh. "And it's really a treasure, but I promise, if I find any gold or diamonds in that old hole, I will make sure to split it with you." His dog was sitting beside him, letting Pastor Ralph scratch his long floppy ears.

"Boys, what did you promise Pastor Ralph you'd do every day of this trip?" Dad asked.

"Read our Bibles," Lenny said confidently.

"Every day," Thomas added.

"King men keep their promises," Dad said. It was a statement they'd heard their dad say many times before.

They took turns giving Pastor Ralph high fives before opening the van doors. Lenny surrendered the shotgun seat to his brother without a fight, and he crawled into the back seat for a nap. Miles of Kansas highway faded away behind them, and they crossed into Colorado in the late afternoon.

Thomas saw the "Welcome to Colorado" sign in the distance and extended his hands as far as he could toward the front window. It was a game their family loved to play on road trips. Dad did the same thing right before they crossed the border.

"I was the first one in Colorado!" Dad said triumphantly.

"Aw, man," Thomas whined. "I can't help it that your arms are so much longer than mine!"

"Let's call it a tie," Dad conceded with a smile.

Lenny popped his head up from the back seat. He'd slept most of the day away.

"We're in Colorado?" he asked, rubbing his eyes and stretching his arms as far as the van roof allowed. "Aren't there mountains in Colorado?"

"Good job remembering your geography, bud," Dad replied. "Yes, Colorado is home to the Rocky Mountains. It's the largest mountain range in North America."[3]

"Well, how come we can't see them?" Lenny asked.

"Colorado is a big state. We'll get to the mountains soon, but we've got another stop first."

They exited the four-lane highway, and Dad steered the van onto a two-lane paved road. Many miles later he navigated them onto a gravel road. White dust flew up from their tires as they bounced along. After what seemed like forever, they veered off the gravel onto a dirt road lined with trees as tall as skyscrapers.

"Where are we going?" Lenny asked expectantly.

"You'll see," Dad replied, glancing at his son from the rearview mirror.

---

3. Rocky Mountain Facts for Kids, Kiddle, January 30, 2023, https://kids.kiddle.co/ Rocky_Mountains.

Thomas was lost in a book and didn't seem to notice the changes in terrain.

Fields filled with grazing cows began to flank them. A cluster of buildings appeared in the distance. Eventually Dad pulled onto a long driveway. The words "Rusty Wheel Ranch" were carved into an archway attached to two columns made up of large, round stones. They bounced and bumped over a cattle guard that marked the ranch's entrance and made their way toward the heart of the Rusty Wheel.

Dad parked the van next to a line of tractors, trucks, and livestock trailers. Some men were training horses in a large corral nearby. A few others were practicing their lasso techniques in the entrance to a huge red barn. They all wore boots, chaps, cowboy hats, and big belt buckles that glinted in the sunshine.

It seemed as if the van had become a time machine and transported them to the Wild West.

Lenny looked down at his basketball jersey, athletic shorts, and flip flops. "I'm not sure we're going to fit in here, Dad," he said.

"Don't worry about it, son," Dad replied, rolling down his window once the dust settled. "They're expecting us, and no one looks like a cowboy on their first day on a dude ranch."

Cattle grazed as far as their eyes could see. In addition to the corral and barn, the property held grain bins, cabins, sheds, chicken coops, watering troughs, and a white farmhouse with a wraparound front porch. The smell of livestock hung in the air, accompanied by constant mooing, clucking, and barking.

"You must be my new farmhands," a voice thundered as a man rode up on a buckskin horse. He brought the horse to a full stop beside the van. The horse was impressive. He tossed his long black mane, causing the brass hardware in his bridle to rattle.

"We are," Dad replied, leaning out of his window. "And you must be Hank."

"In the flesh," the man replied.

He was tall and muscular with skin that was dark and leathered from spending his days in the sun. Hank towered over them as he sat comfortably in his saddle. Thomas noticed that he had the word "hate" tattooed in green ink across the knuckles of his left hand. Thomas turned in his seat and made a face at his brother to try to get him to notice too.

"What?" Lenny asked, oblivious.

"I'll tell you about it later," Thomas whispered, breaking his stare.

"We've got Cabin 3 all set up for you," Hank told them. "You might want to rest up a bit. We ride in two hours."

"Ride what?" Lenny asked, hoping the answer was four-wheelers or ATVs.

"Horses," Hank replied with a laugh. "Didn't your dad tell you? You're going on a cattle drive. You'll be helping the cowboys move a herd of cattle from one spot to another."

The boys looked at their dad waiting for an explanation. Before this trip, Dad had always seemed so predictable, maybe even a little boring. And yet, he'd sent them into an abandoned mine without him, and now he'd signed them up for a cattle drive! They'd never seen this side of him before.

"I told you this was going to be a big adventure," Dad said.

"Let me get my phone." Lenny started to dig into the seat pocket in front of him.

"No, we're not taking any electronics," Dad said firmly. "I don't want you to have any distractions."

"But Daaad," Lenny protested. "I like listening to music when I'm falling asleep. I promise it won't distract me."

"No, bud," Dad repeated. "Look, I'm not even taking mine," he said, tossing it onto the dashboard. "Mom knows we'll be off the grid for a few days. I want you to experience what it's like to live unplugged, just like the old days."

"Pleeeaaase," Lenny pleaded.

"No, son," Dad said, more firmly this time.

"Fine," Lenny said quietly before tucking his phone and headphones back into the seat pocket.

Inside the small cabin they found two stacks of cowboy clothes waiting for them. Their mom had sent them, knowing they would need them, but not wanting to tip them off about what was in store before they left. She'd sent a pair of new blue jeans, a button-up shirt, new socks, and a cowboy hat for each boy. On top of their new hats, they found notes written in their mom's familiar handwriting:

Lenny,

Did you know that I've always wanted to go on a cattle drive? You are going to have so much fun!

There are probably going to be some things about being a cowboy that are really tough. I know you have what it takes to rise to the challenge. I'm praying for you. I miss you.

Love, Momma

Thomas,

I can't wait to hear about your adventure. Remember what to do if you feel afraid: ask Jesus for help. He is always with you. I'm not sure if He ever rode a horse, but He did ride a donkey once. Remind me to tell you that story when you get home. I am praying for you. I miss you. You are so brave!

Love, Momma

"Lenny, go get our boots," Dad said, tossing him the keys. "They aren't cowboy boots, but they'll work."

Lenny did as he was told. After he pulled all six boots out of the back, an idea hit him. He could grab his phone, and no one would know. Without weighing the consequences, he retrieved the phone and stuck it into the side of his shoe. He tucked his headphones into the waist of his shorts and pulled his jersey over them so Dad wouldn't see them. Then he walked back to the cabin.

Dad just doesn't understand how much I love music, Lenny rationalized. *Besides, what's the big deal?*

The boys changed into their new clothes and laced up their boots. Lenny got dressed in the bathroom so he could tuck his phone into his cowboy hat without getting caught. Dad was just finishing lacing up his boots when they heard the sound of a large bell ringing.

"Time to saddle up," Dad announced.

About twenty men were gathered near the horse barn. Most of them looked like cowboys. Later, the boys and their dad found out that the men lived on the ranch year-round. Among the group stood two other families ready to ride. The Gibsons lived in Idaho. The dad was an accountant, and his three boys were Brock, Charlie, and Wyatt, ages sixteen, thirteen, and eleven. The Wilsons were a father-son duo. The dad was a welder, and his son, Tate, had just finished his senior year of high school.

Hank told everyone what to expect. They'd be driving a herd of one thousand cows across thirty miles. The round trip would take four days. Everyone was expected to do their part.

"This isn't a vacation," Hank said. "These are real cows, and this is a real cattle drive. We'll have some fun along the way, but if you want to eat, you better work," he nodded at the boys who had clumped together near their dads.

Everyone was assigned a horse to ride. Lenny got Bullseye, a small black horse with a sleek mane. Thomas's horse was named Buck. It was a buckskin horse with a dark brown mane and tail, like Hank's. Their dad was told to ride Fancy, a black-and-white pinto mare.

It took the newbies a few tries to get the hang of putting their feet in the stirrups and hoisting themselves into the saddle.

They moved their mounts into position and surrounded the herd as Hank instructed them. As the sun began to sink on the horizon, the long train of animals and cowboys started to move.

Thomas struggled to control his horse. When he wanted the animal to go left, it went right. When he wanted to stop, Buck always seemed to want to speed up. With less than a mile under his belt, he was hot, discouraged, and frustrated. As the cattle drive moved forward, he snapped at his brother, argued with his dad, and did a lot of pouting. He did feel bad for the way he was acting, but told himself:

I wouldn't act this way if I wasn't on this stupid cattle drive.

Lenny got an easy horse. I have the worst horse in the bunch.

This isn't even my birthday trip. I don't want to be here! I wish I was home with my friends.

Everyone was always telling Thomas that he was a "good boy." He was his teacher's favorite. She often asked him to help her hand out papers or read with the kids who were struggling. When things got chaotic with his younger siblings, his mom would often look him in the eye and say, "I can always count on you to be a helper, Thomas." Her confidence in him made him feel good about himself.

He tried hard not to make trouble at home or school. He'd never been sent to the principal's office and couldn't remember ever being grounded. He'd been told he was good so many times that it became a part of his identity. Maybe that's why when he heard people talk at church about sin and needing God's forgiveness he always felt like he didn't need that.

The long caravan came to a stop as the last rays of sunshine disappeared. The evening air was cool in Colorado and soon every man was gathered around a roaring fire, bone tired.

The ranch cook was a man named Jake from Memphis, Tennessee. Somehow, despite being miles away from the nearest kitchen, he'd managed to whip up a feast of grilled hamburgers, roasted corn on the cob, and pit beans. Just the smell of all that good food made Thomas's empty stomach twist.

"I could eat a horse," Thomas said, taking his place on the ground, surrounded by the other cowboys.

"Don't say that around Buck," Hank said, nodding up toward the spot nearby where the horses were tied up.

Thomas had only spent a few hours with Hank, but he liked how he treated people. He was a good leader who communicated clear expectations but didn't insist that the boys get it right the first time. He gave everyone a lot of grace.

Thomas suddenly felt brave, emboldened by his first day as a cowboy.

"Hank?" Thomas said.

"Yes, cowboy," Hank replied.

"Why does your hand say 'hate'?" He nodded toward Hank's tattoo.

If Hank minded the question, he didn't show it. And he didn't try to cover up his tattooed knuckles.

"Well, that is a long story. It would probably take several cattle drives for me to tell you all of it. But the short version is that I was a very bad man for a very long time. I even went to prison. I spent most of the first years of my life mad at the world, and I guess I got that word tattooed on my hand so that everyone would know how angry I was."

Thomas tried not to show his shock and resisted the urge to step away from Hank.

"While I was in prison, I realized that all the bad things I'd done didn't just hurt people, they hurt Jesus. I prayed and asked

Jesus to forgive me and to teach me a new way to live. Believe me, I never imagined becoming a cowboy, but here I am. God had a plan for my life that was better than the choices I'd made for myself. I decided not to cover up my tattoo because it often sparks conversations like this one, and I get to tell people about what Jesus has done for me."

Thomas thought about that for a while as he watched the stars appear in the darkening sky like a million tiny Christmas lights. The other cowboys gathered in tight circles, talking quietly. The cattle grazed peacefully in a field nearby. The horses were tied together in a grove of trees and munched on fresh hay.

Thomas was quieter than his older brother because it usually took him a long time to think about what he wanted to say. Hank didn't seem to mind. They just sat together in the silence.

"Hank?" Thomas said again. "I usually make the right decisions. I do what my parents ask me. I get good grades at school. I'm almost never mean to my brothers and sister. I guess, I just don't know why I need Jesus. I mean, I haven't ever even been grounded. I *definitely* haven't done anything that could send me to jail."

"That's good," Hank replied. "But can I ask you some questions?"

"I guess so," Thomas shrugged.

"Have you ever said something you wish you could take back? Maybe during a time when you were angry?"

"Doesn't everybody do that?" Thomas asked.

"Yes," Hank responded. "Have you ever wanted something that someone else had really, really badly?"

Thomas thought for a moment and then said, "Yes, my brother got a phone for his birthday, the exact same one I told Mom I wanted for *my* birthday. I really wish my parents had given me one too."

"I see," Hank replied. "Have you ever taken anything that wasn't yours?"

Thomas froze. A few weeks before they left on this trip, Thomas had stolen a pack of gum. Mom was busy trying to keep his little siblings quiet as she checked out at the grocery store, and she wasn't paying any attention to him. He wanted some gum, and he figured he wasn't hurting anyone by slipping a pink packet into his pocket. How could Hank know about that? "One time," Thomas admitted quietly.

Hank didn't respond for a long time. Thomas felt fidgety.

"Did you know that the Bible says that no one is good?" Hank asked.

"How can that be? I'm a way better kid than most of the kids in my class. Everyone is always telling me what a good kid I am."

"You're a great kid, I can tell that already," Hank assured him. "But none of us are as good as Jesus. He was perfect. He never sinned once. It's like His clothes are so bright white that next to Him, what we're wearing looks dirty and dingy."

Silence settled back in between them. There were so many stars out now that Thomas couldn't begin to count them all. He didn't notice his dad sitting nearby with his head bowed in prayer.

"Hank?" Thomas finally said bravely. "I lost my temper today. I snapped at my dad and my brother even though it wasn't their fault, and I thought some things that I feel bad about."

By now, most of the cattle and several of the cowboys had fallen asleep. The camp felt quiet and loud at the same time. The human noises that were a part of Thomas's everyday life were gone. There were no TVs droning, horns honking, or sirens blaring, but Thomas had never heard so many insects singing. He couldn't see the details of Hank's face in the darkness, but he could tell the older cowboy was looking him in the eyes.

"Did you ever hear the saying 'Nobody's perfect'?" Hank asked.

"Sure."

"Well, that's not true. Jesus *was* perfect, and through His Word He tells us that He wants us to be perfect. We may not all end up in jail, but we all need a way to turn away from our sin. And because God is holy, our sin separates us from Him. We need a way to bridge that gap. Jesus is that way. Like I said, I can tell that you are a great kid, but you aren't a *perfect* kid. That means you need Jesus just as much as I do."

"I've never thought about it that way before," Thomas said.

"Tomorrow is a new day. I know I never run out of reasons to need a fresh start," Hank said, patting Thomas on the back. "For now, whaddya say we do some singing?"

Hank pulled out an old, worn guitar, took a few seconds tuning it, and began to strum. Thomas sat down on a log near his dad who looked at him with kindness in his eyes.

"I love you, son," he said.

"I love you too, Dad," Thomas replied as his mind tried to wrap itself around the conversation he'd just had with Hank.

Surrounded by stars and serenaded by mooing cows and singing cowboys, Thomas realized, for the very first time, that He needed Jesus too.

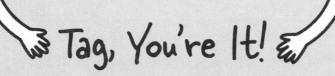

Tag, You're It!

Read Romans 3:23 in your Bible. According to this verse, who has sinned and fallen short of God's glory? **Circle your answer below.**

"Bad" people   People who don't go to church   Everyone

The Bible says that *everyone* has sinned. Have you ever lied? Or cheated on a test? Or taken something that didn't belong to you? Have you ever talked about someone behind their back? Or called someone a mean name? Or done something your mom or dad told you not to? Of course you have. Everyone has. That means that everyone has rebelled against God and said or done things that violate His law.

Now read Romans 6:23. According to this verse, what's the **ultimate punishment we deserve for our sin? Underline one.**

Go to jail, like Hank   Death   To be grounded

It isn't fun to think about, but because God is holy, our sin is deadly serious to Him.

Look up 1 Peter 1:16. Write it out below.

_____

_____

_____

_____

_____

We tend to judge ourselves compared to other people, and that can make us think we're doing okay. There's probably a kid at your school who gets in trouble all the time or someone in your family who struggles to make good choices. You might catch yourself thinking, "I'm glad I'm not like him!" But the Bible teaches us to stop using other people as our measuring stick and to start considering how our lives measure up against God's holiness. Since God is perfect and we aren't, we all fall short, like a runner who can never make it across the finish line or a basketball player who can never score a point.

That's like a dark cloud, but here's the silver lining. Jesus died to make a way for our sins to be forgiven and our hearts to be made new. We deserve to be punished for our sin, but because He loves us so much, He offers us a free gift—the most wonderful gift anyone could ever give us—forgiveness! The Bible calls this grace. That's the good news of the gospel.

Before you read the next chapter and discover what Lenny and Thomas experience on the cattle drive, take some time to talk to a grown-up about the gospel. It could be your mom or dad, your pastor, or another grown-up you respect from church. Tell them what you've learned, and ask any questions that might be lingering in your mind. Be sure to tell them if you've never asked Jesus to forgive you of your sins and you want to take that important step now.

LIE #3:
"No one needs to know about my sin."
TRUTH:
Telling your story to someone and admitting your sin sets you free.

The life of a cowboy was challenging . . . and exciting!

The days started early with eggs and bacon cooked in a big cast-iron skillet that Jake placed on the hot coals of the campfire. He didn't have to worry about what to do with leftovers. The hungry boys and their dads gobbled up every bite as they watched the sun rise, painting streaks of red, orange, and pink across the Colorado sky. Then, everyone worked together to pack up camp, coax the cows into formation, round up any stragglers, and start moving.

Lenny and Thomas were living every boy's dream. No homework! No rooms to clean! Just long days outside with their dad, surrounded by new friends.

Every few hours, Hank would call the drive to a halt so that the cows could drink or rest.

"You guys want to have a slingshot competition?" Tate Wilson, the welder's son, asked the first morning of the drive.

"What's that?" thirteen-year-old Charlie Gibson responded.

Charlie and his brothers lived in a crowded neighborhood in Boise with plenty of houses close by. These houses had lots of windows they knew better than to break, and they'd never owned a slingshot.

Tate pulled a homemade slingshot and a bunch of rubber bands from his back pocket. "City boys!" he said with a smile while he gave Charlie a playful jab in the ribs.

"It's easy," he continued. "You just find a stick with a Y, like this one." He held up his slingshot and used his finger to trace the Y shape of the wood. "Then, you grab a rubber band, tie it onto each of the two forks, pull it back, and *snap*, you're ready to fire."

"Cool!" Lenny and Charlie said at the same time.

Build Your Own Slingshot

1. Find a sturdy stick with a Y shape (also known as a fork).

2. Near the top of the right and left branches of the Y, carve small V-shaped notches. Your rubber band will rest in these notches.

3. Give a tug to both branches of the Y to make sure they are strong enough to withstand pressure.

4. Cut a wide rubber band. The ones around broccoli and asparagus are good for this. A great reason to eat more vegetables!

5. Tie each end to the stick at the notches. Your rubber band should have some tension, but not be strung tight. If necessary, you can tie two rubber bands together.

6. Pull the rubber band back to make sure everything is secure.

7. Find a small stone or nut.

8. Place it in the middle of the rubber band. Keep it secure by pinching it with your fingers.

9. Set up some empty cans or containers for targets.

10. Aim, pull back, and release.

11. Yell something cool like "Fire!" or "Bombs away!"

Thomas and Lenny had more experience with a slingshot than their new friends from Idaho. They'd each received one from their favorite uncle a couple of Christmases ago. In the summer, they'd load them with small rocks and fire them at the old rusty shed in their backyard.

Ping!
Plink!
Kerplunk!

The rocks made a cool sound when they pelted the metal shed walls.

"I have a slingshot at home," Thomas told the group. "But I've never made my own."

"No time like right now!" Lenny announced. He always took on new challenges with confidence.

The boys fanned out to look for the perfect Y-shaped sticks. Soon enough the young cowboys were back in a circle, with a pile of sticks and stones in the middle. Some of the sticks needed minor modifications: a little bark peeled here, a twig shortened there. They all needed notches to help the rubber bands stay in place. Lenny had brought his pocketknife along, and the whittling skills he learned from Pastor Ralph came in handy.

Soon, each of the young cowboys had a working slingshot of his own. Charlie grabbed six used cans from the chuck wagon and placed them in a line. "I've got an idea," he announced. "First one to hit their can wins *and* gets bragging rights until the next stop."

"Slingshot King! I like the sound of that," Lenny announced.

"When *I* win," Tate joked, "you'll have to call me the GOAT, 'cuz I'm the greatest slingshot shooter of all time!"

"Sorry," Charlie's older brother, Brock, said. "I may be a 'city boy,' but I can't let your head get that big. I'm in!"

The boys each grabbed a handful of small smooth stones and filled their pockets.

Dad, Hank, and some of the other cowboys wandered over to see what the boys were so excited about.

"Ah, I see we've got a little competition going on," Hank said. "Tell you what, I will sweeten the deal. Whoever knocks over their can first, gets bragging rights *and* no K.P. duty at lunch."

K.P. stood for "kitchen patrol." The six boys were in charge of washing up the dishes after every meal and helping Jake get the chuck wagon ready for the next leg of the journey. It wasn't exactly hard work, but they liked the idea of lingering by the fire and watching their new friends do all the scrubbing. "You're on!" Charlie's younger brother, Wyatt, exclaimed. He was the youngest of the three Gibson brothers but just as tall as his brothers. Normally an outgoing kid, he'd been pretty quiet on the cattle drive so far. He wasn't sure the cowboy life was for him, but the slingshot competition had awakened his competitive spirit and suddenly he was as loud and talkative as all the other boys.

Tate drew a long line in the dirt with the toe of his boot.

"We gotta stay behind this line," he announced.

The young cowboys stood behind the line. Each one placed a stone in the middle of the rubber band. On Hank's cue, they pulled back and let them fly.

Whizz!
Whoosh!
Kerplunk!

Lenny's first shot sailed high over the target and landed with a thud against the chuck wagon. Thomas's made it about halfway to the row of cans and then took a nosedive into the dirt. Wyatt's dropped straight to the ground as soon as he released the tension. Charlie's stone hit a can, but it was the one on the opposite end from where he was aiming. Brock's and Tate's stones fell to the ground just before hitting a can.

"This is tougher than I thought!" Wyatt admitted.

"No kidding!" Thomas replied. "You'll get the hang of it," he added.

"If at first you don't succeed . . . what do we do, boys?" Dad asked.

Instinctively, Lenny and Thomas replied, "Try, try again." Ever since they were little, their dad had trained them not to give up easily. Though they often whined and sometimes argued with their dad, they had both seen their dad stick with it when a job was hard, like the time he taught Thomas to ride a bike despite more than a few failed attempts.

Each boy loaded another stone and pulled back on their rubber bands.

"Ready, aim, fire!" Hank hollered.

This time, Thomas's shot went wild
and nearly knocked off the hat
of another cowboy.

"Sorry about that!" Thomas shouted.

"No problem, partner," the cowboy replied,
straightening his hat.

Most of the shots were closer to the line of cans than they had
been in round one, but no one was bragging anymore. A look of
concentration fell over Thomas's face just like it had in the mine.
Lenny was as confident as usual. A wide grin showed how much
he was enjoying the competition. After several more rounds and
lots of encouragement (along with some occasional heckling),
finally the crowd heard the sound they'd been waiting for:

Ping!

It was Lenny who finally hit his mark.

The cowboys who were watching yelled "Whooooeee" and "Atta
boy," though there wasn't a lot of time to celebrate.

"These cows won't move themselves. We'd better get moving,"
Hank said. He gave Lenny a big pat on the back. "You sure

picked a good day to get out of K.P. duty. Jake said we're having sloppy joes for lunch."

"Sloppy joes means messy dishes," Jake added with a wink.

The boys gathered up the cans.

"Don't get too used to being on top," Tate joked. "I want a rematch at the next stop. Deal?"

"Deal!" The boys agreed as they each saddled their horse and settled in for the next stretch of the ride.

Tag, You're It!

In the last chapter you read in Romans 3:23 that "everyone has sinned." How do you define "sin"? **Write down your answer below.**

_____

_____

_____

Romans 3:23 gives us a clue about what sin is, but you might have missed it. Let's break this verse up into two parts:

Part 1: "For everyone has sinned."

Maybe you've already learned in school how to identify the 5 Ws in a sentence: who, what, when, where, and why. The first part of this verse gives us the **what** and the **who**.

What = sin

Who = _____

Everyone you know has sinned. If you're wondering about the *why* of this truth, think back to what you learned about Satan in chapter 1:

- Satan is a villain. (Remember Genesis 3?)
- He deceives God's children into thinking that God's rules don't count.
- When we fall for his lies, we are drawn toward sin.

Still not sure you know what sin is? The answer is waiting for you in the second half of Romans 3:23. Trace the words below.

We all fall short of
God's glorious standard.
(Romans 3:23)

According to Scripture, sin is falling short of God's perfect standard. That's another way of saying falling short of God's holiness.

Holiness = perfection

God has never lied (Numbers 23:19; Titus 1:2; Hebrews 6:18). He has never taken something that didn't belong to Him. (Everything belongs to Him according to Deuteronomy 10:14.) He isn't selfish, mean, or hurtful.

Look up Psalm 18:30. How does it describe God's way?

_____

_____

In the center of the target below, write the word holy.

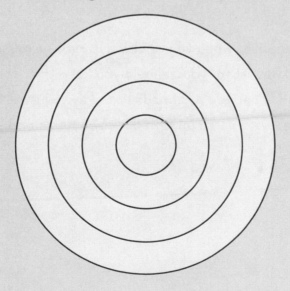

Remember, holy = perfect. God is perfect, but we are not. Like when the boys couldn't hit the cans with their slingshots, we miss the mark He has for us. We sin. Following Jesus isn't really about being the perfect basketball player, the perfect friend, or the perfect kid. It's about aiming for the standard God has set for our lives in His Word.

Remember how Thomas's rock hit another cowboy in the hat? That's a good picture for sin. When we don't live like God asks us to, it impacts other people, and sometimes it hurts them (and us). That doesn't make us feel good, but remember the gospel? The Good News is that Jesus took the punishment we deserved for sin so that we don't have to.

Because you love Jesus, not because you're trying to convince Him to love you (He already loves you SO MUCH!), you will want to live like He calls you to live in His Word.

But what happens when you've blown it—you've missed the target God has set for you? Should you keep that a secret so no one ever finds out you've sinned? Is it okay to just tell God and no one else? Let's catch up with our cowboys to find out.

. . .

After a long morning, it was time to stop for lunch.
As promised, Jake served up huge helpings of sloppy joes
with homemade kettle chips and giant dill pickles.

As his friends cleared and cleaned the dirty dishes, Lenny
should have been enjoying the extra free time, but he just
couldn't relax. He felt mad and sad at the same time. He
couldn't sit still.

"Something bothering you, bud?" Dad asked.

"I'm fine!" Lenny snapped.

"You don't seem fine," Dad replied. "You can either tell me
what's going on or turn your attitude around. . . . your choice,"
he added before giving his son a pat on the back. Then Dad
walked over to see how he could help the other cowboys,
leaving Lenny alone with his thoughts.

That just made it worse! Something was bothering Lenny.
All he could think about was the phone he had stashed in his
hat. Dad made it very clear that Lenny wasn't supposed to
bring it along, but Lenny had disobeyed.

"What's the big deal?" he muttered under his breath while he
whittled a small stick.

But he knew what the big deal was. His dad had gone to a lot of trouble to plan this trip. Lenny knew that his parents probably saved money for a long time to make it possible. And Dad had been so great about everything. Still, when he gave Lenny one simple rule . . .

"We're not taking any electronics.
I don't want you to have any distractions."

. . . Lenny had ignored his dad's instructions and disobeyed.

Now, Lenny felt miserable. He was terrified that his dad would find out and be mad at him, so he had to constantly be thinking about how to keep his phone hidden. Plus, it didn't even work out here. There were no plug-ins to charge it, so the battery was now dead.

To make matters worse, Lenny knew that he hadn't just let his dad down. He'd learned in church that "Honor your father and mother" was one of the Ten Commandments (Exodus 20:12). That meant he'd sinned.

A little voice inside his heart kept nudging him to tell his dad what he'd done, but he ignored it.

It's not hurting anyone.
I don't want to hurt my dad's feelings.
God already knows . . . isn't that enough?
I don't want to ruin this great trip.

Those thoughts swirled round and round in Lenny's head like a Texas tornado. No matter how hard he tried, he just couldn't shake his guilt *or* his feeling that he should tell someone what he had done.

Tag, You're It!

Have you ever had an experience like Lenny's? Has there been a time when you've sinned and the fear of someone finding out made you feel upset? **Write about it below.**

_____

_____

God has given you a conscience. It works like an inner voice helping you know the difference between right and wrong. He's also given you the Bible to show you in black and white what God wants you to do, like love Him and others. You also should obey your parents and do what God wants you to do, or *not* do what He doesn't want you to do, like lie or steal. He has already given you everything you need to follow Him (2 Peter 1:3).

So, when something inside of you feels sad or angry about your sin, that's great news! It means God is working in your heart. He has promised He will forgive you when you tell Him what you've done (1 John 1:9). That's true even if you make the same mistake a million times.

God also wants you to tell other wise followers of Jesus when you sin so that they can pray with you and help you make better choices next time.

Write out James 5:16 below.

_____

_____

Who does this verse tell us to confess our sins to?

_____

_____

Only Jesus has the power to forgive sins, so He should be the one you tell first when you've sinned. But He also asks you to tell someone else. This isn't a punishment. It's a gift! Confessing to someone you love and trust frees you from carrying the heavy weight of sin by yourself. And when you know someone is watching, it's easier to say "no" to sin the next time you're tempted.

Covering up sins and mistakes is a hard habit to break. Right now, you might just be sneaking an extra cookie after bedtime

or lying about it when you break something that didn't belong
to you. But as you grow older, your temptations will grow too,
and you may find yourself trying to hide your sin from God and
from those who love you.

Break the pattern now. God's Word doesn't invite you to tell
others when you've made a mistake to embarrass or shame
you, but so that other people who love you and love Jesus can
help you.

Before you turn to the next chapter, take time to pray. Ask the
Lord to remind you if there are areas of your life where you've
sinned and that He wants to forgive. Then talk to your mom,
dad, older siblings, teachers, or pastors about it. Ask them to
help you turn from sin and aim for God's best in the future.

LIE #4:

"God is always mad at me."

TRUTH:

God forgives!

LIE:
God is always
mad at me.

As the sun rose on the fourth day of the cattle drive, Lenny ate his breakfast extra fast so that he'd have time for one more slingshot competition before K.P. duty. Thomas stayed by the campfire. He sat close to his dad, but didn't say much.

Dad always seemed to know when something was bothering one of his boys, but he'd learned that Thomas didn't like it when someone asked him what was the matter. Thomas would usually open up if Dad just sat with him in silence for a while. That's what he did that morning. Surrounded by beautiful scenery and listening to the sounds of a thousand mooing cows, Dad just sat close to his boy, watching the last campfire of this part of their journey smolder, silently praying for his son.

Thomas picked up sticks and started building a small cabin on the ground like he often did with LEGO bricks at home. Dad scooted closer and started adding sticks to the miniature frame.

"Dad?" Thomas said, finally breaking the silence.

"Yeah, son?"

"I've been thinking a lot about what Hank told me when we started this trip, that no one is good but God."

"I remember."

"I see what he means," Thomas said, as he began adding a roof to his building. "All these years I've thought of myself as a good kid, but I do things I shouldn't sometimes, and I think things I shouldn't *a lot* of the time. Like just this morning, I was jealous of Lenny because it seems so easy for him to make friends. I wish I was more like that."

"Lenny does have lots of friends," Dad agreed. "But you're a lot like your momma. She just has two or three really close friends, and she's cautious about making new friends. There's nothing wrong with that."

"I know, Dad," Thomas said, digging the toe of his boot into the dirt. "But I'm pretty sure God doesn't want me to be jealous of my brother for being so friendly."

"I guess you're right," Dad said.

"The thing is, now that I understand what sin really is, I can see that I'm not as good as I thought I was, and that really bothers me. I guess I just feel like God must be really mad at me."

LIE:
God is always
mad at me.

"I see," Dad said.

"And Dad?"

"Yes, son."

"I haven't been reading my Bible. I know I told you and Pastor Ralph I would, and I want to . . . I really do . . . I dunno, I've just filled my time with other things, I guess. I feel like I've let God down," Thomas said quietly. A tear rolled down his face and onto his T-shirt.

"That must be a heavy weight to carry," Dad said. "Feeling like God is always mad at you, I mean."

"I guess so," Thomas replied. "I don't like it when *anyone* is mad at me, Dad. Especially God."

Hank interrupted their conversation by yelling "Move out!" It was time for the cows and cowboys to make the final push of the drive.

. . .

All one thousand cows were delivered to the Jubilee Ranch late in the afternoon on the fourth day of the drive. The cowboys were happy, hungry, and tired.

"You ready to give up middle school and become a full-time cattle rancher?" Hank joked as Lenny closed the gate on the last pen of livestock.

"Not quite," Lenny smiled. "But I don't think my friends will ever believe that I spent some time as a real cowboy."

"Just show 'em those calluses," Hank advised. Small white patches of rough skin had appeared on all the boys' hands from roping and riding. "You can't get those from playing video games," he added, tossing Lenny a lasso.

Trucks and trailers were waiting for them at the Jubilee. They loaded the horses into the trailers and piled into the trucks for the thirty-mile drive back to the Rusty Wheel.

"I can't wait to take a hot shower," Thomas announced.

"I can't wait to take these boots off," Lenny said.

"I can't wait to call your momma!" Dad said. "Do you think she misses us? I sure miss her."

"Nothing against Jake," Lenny said, "but I miss Momma's cooking. I hope she has a big batch of chocolate chip cookies waiting for us when we get home."

"Or peanut butter cookies," Thomas replied.

LIE:
God is always
mad at me.

"Or chocolate pie," Dad added.

"This conversation is making me even hungrier," Thomas said.

Dad drove a rusty blue pickup truck back to the ranch. The boys sat beside him on the vinyl bench seat. A faded leather tassel swung from the cracked rearview mirror. Soon enough they were bumping across the cattle guard of the Rusty Wheel.

"Wow! Thirty miles sure goes by faster when you're on wheels instead of hooves," Thomas said. That made everyone chuckle.

There was a lot of work to do back at the Rusty Wheel. The chuck wagon supplies needed to be put away. The horses needed to be brushed and given fresh hay. The saddles needed to be cleaned and stored. The boys had never worked this hard in their entire lives. They were covered in dust and sweat, but they were happy. It felt good to hear Hank say, "Well done, cowboys."

All the cowboys, including the families who just finished their first drive, gathered in a circle. A tall wooden cross stood on a hill nearby. A couple of cowboys pulled guitars from beat-up cases and began to strum. Most of the songs were ones Lenny and Thomas had learned in church, like "How Great Thou Art," "It is Well with My Soul," and their momma's favorite, "Amazing Grace."

As roasting forks and marshmallows were passed around, Hank shared the story he had told Thomas on the first night of the drive with the rest of the group. "I do this because I love being outdoors. I love meeting new people and I love being in the saddle," Hank said. "But this is really about finding a way to share Jesus' love with people like you."

The elms had been rustling in the breeze, but when Hank started to share, even the trees seemed to go still and listen to Hank's story.

LIE:
God is always
mad at me.

Lenny and Thomas had heard about Jesus' love many times from their parents. They'd attended Vacation Bible Schools and church camps. Lenny had written Philippians 4:13 with a permanent marker on his basketball shoes last year just like his favorite NBA player.

Hank's story was familiar. But being away from the distractions of their normal lives and listening to Hank talk under a sky filled with millions of bright stars, their hearts felt stirred in a new way.

Lenny could not stop thinking about the phone still stashed under his hat. At first, he'd wanted to do things *his way*, no matter what his dad said. Then, he just didn't want his dad to find out that he'd disobeyed. Now, listening to Hank share about God's love and grace, he just wanted to be free from his guilt and shame.

"I need to tell you something, Dad," he whispered, not wanting to distract from Hank's story.

"Does it have anything to do with the phone that you've been hiding in that hat of yours?" Dad asked, looking Lenny square in the eye.

"You knew?" Lenny asked.

"The whole time," Dad said firmly.

"Aren't you mad?" Lenny asked.

"A little," Dad admitted.

"Why didn't you say something?"

"Good question," Dad replied. "Why do you think I didn't say something?"

"Um . . ." Lenny stalled. "Because you wanted me to fess up on my own?"

"I guess that's part of it," Dad replied.

Lenny hoped his dad would say more. When he didn't, Lenny prayed silently for God to help him know what to say. "I know you want me to obey you," Lenny said slowly. "But I think you want me to *want* to obey you. Right?"

"I never really thought about it that way," Dad said as he picked at a mosquito bite on his arm. "But yes, I do want you to want to obey me because I want you to trust me." He paused. "Anything else coming to your mind, son?"

"This may sound weird," Lenny said, "but it seems the way I respond to you has to do with the way I respond to God." He paused. "I mean, He wants me to trust Him too. When I disobey Him, I guess I'm kind of saying that I don't trust Him. Does that make sense?"

LIE:
God is always
mad at me.

"Makes perfect sense," Dad said. "It *is* important for you to trust me as your earthly father, but it's even more important that you learn to trust your heavenly Father. I wanted you to tell me because you understood that disobeying me and then covering it up is a sin, not just because you didn't want to get in trouble."

"Am I in trouble?" Lenny asked.

"Every night when you thought I was asleep, I was paying attention to you. I saw how hard it was for you to fall asleep and I knew this was what was bothering you. I'd say you've punished yourself enough for both of us."

"How can you spy on me with your eyes closed?" Lenny asked.

"Dads have their ways," he replied.

"I'm sorry, Dad," Lenny said. "I told God I was sorry too."

"Then consider it forgiven. Let's listen to Hank. I love this part of his story."

Hank was telling the group about how he gave his life to Jesus while he was in prison. Cowboys don't usually cry, but they could hear emotion in the sound of his voice.

"Jesus died on a cross a lot like that one," he said, pointing to the cross on the hill. "He did that for two reasons: because

He loves us so much and because He wanted to take the punishment we deserve for our sin. God has given me so much grace, and before you head back to where you came from, I want you to know that His grace is for you too. Would you pray with me?"

Every cowboy took off his hat and bowed his head. Hank led the group in a simple prayer of gratitude for a successful cattle drive. The boys could tell Hank had a lump in his throat as he thanked Jesus for going to the cross for his sin. After he said "Amen," the cowboys began strumming their guitars again. The boys started roasting marshmallows. Charlie even put a marshmallow in his slingshot and fired it at his brothers. Everyone had a good laugh about that.

• • •

Back in Cabin 3, Dad, Lenny, and Thomas were bone tired.

"I think even my hair is tired," Thomas joked.

"Maybe that's why it looks so funny," Lenny teased.

LIE:
God is always
mad at me.

Lenny was the first to fall asleep. Soon his breathing changed from shallow to deep and slow. But Thomas's sheets rustled as he tried to get comfortable in the bed beside his brother.

"Thomas?" Dad whispered into the darkness. "I've been thinking about what you said about God being mad at you."

"Me too," Thomas said, settling in.

"Can you think of a time when I got mad at you?"

"Hmm . . . how about the time I borrowed your good hammer without asking and then left it in the rain," Thomas replied after giving it some thought.

"I'd forgotten about that," Dad said with a chuckle. "I think I was mad at you when I found my hammer all rusted up. But have I stayed mad at you all this time?"

"No, and I'm glad," Thomas murmured. His eyes felt as heavy as saddlebags. "I *hate* it when you're mad at me."

"Why do you think I didn't stay mad? I mean, you did ruin my best hammer," Dad said.

"Because you love me?"

"Was that a question?" Dad asked. "Do you know that I love you?"

"Yeah, Dad," Thomas replied. "I know that you love me."

Lenny rolled over in his bunk, mumbled something in his sleep about slingshotting flaming marshmallows, and then went quiet again.

"Well," Dad continued, "the more important question is, how do you know that *God* loves you?"

Thomas thought about this as he tried to stifle a yawn. "Well, because He says so in His Word. I started reading my Bible again this morning, like I promised I would. John 3:16 says that the way God showed His love for the world was by sending Jesus to die for us. I live in the world and so God's love is for *me*," Thomas said.

Thomas was obviously getting sleepy. His words came out as slow as maple syrup over a tall stack of buttermilk pancakes.

"You know how else you can know?" Dad asked.

"How, Dad?"

"You can know that Jesus loves you because He went to the cross for you. He endured pain and rejection and loneliness for you. He wouldn't do that if He didn't love you very much. And you can know that God's not mad at you because all His anger at sin was poured out on Jesus on the cross."

"That's hard to understand," Thomas admitted.

LIE:
God is always
mad at me.

"You're right, but that doesn't make it untrue. It's good to want to please God. It's good to tell Him you're sorry when you do something wrong. But because God loves you, and because Jesus took the punishment you deserve, you don't have to be worried that He's mad at you all the time. Just tell Him you're sorry, accept His grace, and say thank you."

"Kind of like you and the hammer."

"You got it, kiddo."

"Thanks, Dad. I feel better," Thomas said after a long moment of silence. "Dad? . . . Dad?"

The sounds of Dad's snoring soon filled the cabin.

Thomas drifted off to sleep too. In his dreams, he was on another wild adventure with Buck.

Tag, You're It!

When you think about God, what words come to mind? **Circle your answers from the group of words below.**

Angry   Gentle   Distant

Uptight   Fun   Friendly   Irritated

Kind   Boring   Mysterious

Mean   Easygoing   Strange   Happy

Loving   Annoyed   Unpredictable

Can you think about a time you were disciplined for making a mistake? **Write a few sentences about it.**

_____

_____

_____

_____

_____

LIE:
God is always
mad at me.

Trace Proverbs 3:12 and Hebrews 12:6 below.

"For the LoRD corrects those he loves,
just as a father corrects a child in whom he
delights." (Proverbs 3:12)

"For the LoRD disciplines those he loves,
and he punishes each one he accepts as his child."
(Hebrews 12:6)

Look at those two verses again. **Go back and circle *who* God disciplines.**

According to God's Word, discipline is an act of love. Your heavenly Father punishes you when you miss His mark, just like an earthly father punishes his son for disobedience.

No one likes discipline. It usually feels painful at the time. But a good dad can't let his children do whatever they want, or they will end up in danger. In the same way, God cannot let His children rebel against the guidelines He's placed in His Word. His rules are there to protect you. **God's discipline does not mean He is mad at you. It means He loves you.**

Look up 1 John 1:9 and write it out below.

_____

_____

_____

God has promised that when you confess your sin to Him, He will forgive you; and **God always keeps His promises.** You don't have to worry that He's still mad at you about something you did a long time ago once you've told Him about it and asked for forgiveness. Isn't that amazing news?!

Micah 7:19 makes this bold promise: "Once again you will have compassion on us. You will trample our sins under your feet and **throw them into the depths of the ocean!**"

One way to think of that is to imagine that once you've asked God to forgive you for something, He hurls your sin into the deepest parts of the ocean . . . and He doesn't own scuba gear! He's not going to dive down and drag those sins up because He's mad at you. Just like how Thomas's dad forgot that his son had ruined his best hammer, God's forgiveness is so complete, it's as if He's forgotten it completely.

Is there something you're worried God is mad at you about? Ask His forgiveness, then tell someone who can pray for you and help you make a better choice next time. Then let it go. God has thrown it into the deepest part of the sea.

LIE #5:
"Girls rule, boys drool!"

TRUTH:
The differences between guys and girls are God's idea.

"Cannonball!" Thomas announced before bouncing off the diving board and into the pool.

Dad and the boys had checked into a hotel for the night. The sliding glass door of their room opened onto a small courtyard with a kidney-shaped pool in the center. The boys wasted no time getting wet, barely stopping to put on their swim trunks before jumping in. They spent the next hours playing Marco Polo and competing with each other in a variety of made-up diving techniques.

Dad announced the scores for each dive from his spot in a deck chair. "10!" . . . "7.5!" . . . "Negative 2!"

The scores didn't matter. They were all having fun.

At one point in the evening, another family rolled out their towels on the deck chairs beside the Kings. The mom pulled a paperback from her pool bag and quickly got lost in its pages while the dad and Mr. King struck up a conversation about the trips they were on and what they each did for work. The family had two daughters who looked a little younger than Lenny and Thomas. One had long, blond hair braided down her back. The other had copper red hair piled in a messy bun on top of her head.

While the boys splashed and took turns dunking each other, the girls sat on the side of the pool silently gliding their feet through the water and talking. And while Dad had to take frequent pauses in his conversation with the other dad to say things like, "Not so rough, boys," and "Quit horsing around," and "No, you cannot push your brother off the diving board just because you're bigger," the girls' parents didn't get on their case once as they sat like statues at the pool's edge.

"You've got your hands full," the boys heard the other dad say to their dad. It was a line they'd heard strangers say too many times to count.

Momma's typical response was, "Yes, and so is my heart." Her boys knew she meant it, but why did everyone seem to feel the need to talk about raising boys like it was some form of torture? They weren't *trying* to be a handful.

It was the double cannonball that did them in. Lenny and Thomas decided to jump in at the same time to see if they could create a tidal wave. Turns out, they could—at least a mini one. Water splashed out of the pool onto the mom's book. Lenny and Thomas swam over to the side of the pool where the parents were gathered and started spitting pool water at each other.

"I'm so sorry!" Dad exclaimed, offering her a towel. "Boys, you owe this lady an apology," he added, looking at them.

"Sorry," Thomas said.

"Yeah, we didn't mean to get you wet," Lenny added sincerely.

"It's fine," she said flatly as her lips clenched together in a tight line. "Let's go, girls!" she added.

Dad dropped the towel he'd been holding onto the concrete pool deck and turned toward his sons.

As the family walked toward their room, Thomas heard the mom say, "I'm sure glad we had girls!"

Dad clearly heard it and crossed his arms. The boys couldn't tell if he was frustrated with them or with the lady's comment.

"Sorry, Dad," Thomas said sincerely, as he popped out of the water and began drying off with the towel his dad dropped. Lenny dove underwater one last time and swam to the wide stairs at the edge of the pool. As he came around to where his brother was sitting, he said, "We weren't trying to cause trouble."

"I know you weren't, bud," Dad replied. "But next time, send your splash in the other direction, okay?"

Their parents had always encouraged them to do the things boys seem to love to do: climb trees, catch bugs, build forts, wrestle with each other.

"All of boyhood is one continuous war game," Momma liked to say when she got in the crossfire of her sons' latest dart gun battle. But she never said it in a way that made them feel bad about wanting to pretend they were soldiers at war or a SWAT team working together to take out the bad guy.

"Dad?" Thomas asked. "Are girls better than boys?"

"Better how, son?" Dad asked.

"I dunno." Thomas shrugged. "Just better."

"We weren't trying to cause any trouble," Lenny repeated. "But those girls barely even made a ripple in the water. The same thing happens at school. If someone gets in trouble, it's almost always a boy. Girls just seem better at being quiet and sitting still."

"Why do you think that is?" Dad asked.

Thomas shrugged again. "We're just different, I guess."

"You know what they say at school?" Lenny interjected. "Girls rule, and boys drool." He stuck out his tongue and acted like he was drooling.

"That saying has been around since I was a kid," Dad said.

"You do drool on your pillow sometimes," Thomas teased.

"I don't think that's what that means," Lenny said, suddenly serious. "It's like people think boys are dumb or something."

"Did you ever hear this one?" Dad asked. "Boys go to Jupiter to get more stupider . . ."

"Girls go to college to get more knowledge!" Thomas finished his dad's sentence.

"That's what I'm talking about," Lenny said, clearly frustrated.

"It's not like all boys are dumb and all girls are smart. I have this one teacher, Mrs. Williams. She loooves all the girls in her class. She's always telling them 'Good job' and 'I'm so proud of you,' but the boys in her class can't seem to do anything right. A couple of weeks ago I got in trouble for chewing too loudly."

Thomas thought about telling Lenny that he *did* chew like a horse, but he thought better of it. His brother was making a good point. Why *did* people seem to think that girls were better than boys?

"What about this one?" he asked. "Girls are made of sugar and spice and everything nice. Boys are made of snips and snails and puppy dog tails. What does that even mean? It sure sounds like girls are made of good stuff and boys . . . aren't."

"Did I ever tell you that I always wanted a brother?" Dad asked. "Instead, I grew up with one sister, your Aunt Sissy. She wasn't perfect, no one is, but when we were kids, she got in a lot less trouble than I did. I tended to be rowdy. I liked to play cowboys and capture the flag . . . those kinds of games. She was more interested in quiet activities. She loved to draw, and that girl could read for hours! No one had to teach us to operate differently, it's just how God made us."

"You're saying girls are better because that's how God made them?" Lenny asked.

"That's not what I'm saying," Dad said. "Your momma and I have a lot in common, but boy, are we different!"

"Like what?" Thomas asked.

"She smells better," Lenny joked.

"No doubt about that," Dad said. "One thing that comes to mind is that your mom needs to hear that I love her every day. She likes to hear those words from you too. Love is important, but I want to know that she respects me, that she believes I have what it takes. I know how much it means to you when she tells you that she believes in you. It's not that one way is right and the other way is wrong. We're just different, and that's a good thing."

Lenny stared off into the distance. The past year or so, he'd stopped thinking of girls as annoying pests to chase at recess. There was one girl at church, Kendra, that made his stomach tie up in knots every time he saw her. She was pretty, and nice, and easy to talk to, but she was kind of confusing too. Lenny couldn't tell if she liked him back or not, or even if he wanted her to.

"Do you remember when we talked about Adam and Eve?" Dad asked.

Both boys nodded.

125

"Yeah, and they were both God's idea, so it's not like Adam was a mistake and God had to make Eve to fix it," Lenny said.

"It's not like God made Adam and Adam," Thomas piped up, finishing his brother's thought. "God made men and women different from the beginning."

"Right," Dad said. "Boys and girls both have value to God, but that doesn't mean we're the same."

It was getting late, and the pull of the pool was strong.

Lenny walked over to the diving board and climbed up. Dad quietly moved backward, preparing for the coming splash. Thomas missed his dad's cue and stayed on the side of the pool wrapped in a white hotel towel.

"I bet most girls wouldn't do *this*!" Lenny announced from the diving board before doing a spectacular belly flop.

"A perfect 10," Dad announced as Lenny emerged from the water with a red belly.

"I can beat that!" Thomas said as he raced toward the diving board, dropping his now-soaked towel.

"Boys will be boys," Dad said and laughed. "And I sure am glad."

Tag, You're It!

What makes a boy a boy and a girl a girl? Besides the differences in their bodies, there are differences in the ways we think and respond to the world around us.

Read Genesis 1:27 below. Circle who is made in God's image.

So God created human beings in his own image.
In the image of God he created them;
male and female he created them.

Both men and women are made by God and both bear the image of God. That means that boys *and* girls have tremendous God-given value. Both boys *and* girls have something to show the world about who God is. That's two important things boys *and* girls have in common:

1. They both matter to God.
2. They both bear God's image.

But that doesn't mean that boys and girls are exactly the same. If you have a sister, then you probably already know that she doesn't always operate just like you do. She likely has different interests and strengths and may respond to the world around her in ways that you don't. **Different isn't bad.** In fact, God looked at the unique ways He created Adam and Eve and declared it was very good (Genesis 1:27, 31).

In the New Testament, there is a letter that the apostle Paul wrote to his young friend Titus. Paul told Titus to help people live like God made them to live. He gave Titus a list of some of the qualities godly men and women should have. **Read Paul's words below. As you read, circle the virtues Paul told Titus to teach to men.**

As for you, Titus, promote the kind of living that reflects wholesome teaching. Teach the older men to exercise self-control, to be worthy of respect, and to live wisely. They must have sound faith and be filled with love and patience.

Similarly, teach the older women to live in a way that honors God. They must not slander others or be heavy drinkers. Instead, they should teach others what is good. These older women must train the younger women to love their husbands and their children, to live wisely and be pure, to work in their homes, to do good, and to be submissive to their husbands. Then they will not bring shame on the word of God. (Titus 2:1–5)

Do you know a godly man who lives out the virtues you just underlined? Do you know a godly woman who lives out the virtues listed in this passage? Write their names below.

_____

_____

While men and women are both called to show love and be strong, that looks different in the unique roles God has designed us for. Titus 2 is just one of many passages that make it clear: **God hasn't made everyone the same.** Boys and girls are God's idea! And what a good idea it is.

Instead of trying to decide who is better or feeling frustrated because you don't operate like the girls you know, ask God to bring wise men into your life to show you what being a good guy looks like. Pay attention to the stories in Scripture of men who God used to protect His people, stop wicked rulers, and tell people what He is like. Pray and ask Him to help you understand how He made you so that you can show the world who He is.

LIE #6:
"I don't need friends."

TRUTH:
You need battle buddies.

As Dad and the boys loaded their suitcases into the van the next morning, Dad pulled out a green plastic tub like the ones Mom used to store their Christmas ornaments. This one wasn't full of colorful bulbs or tiny baby footprints pressed into plaster. When Dad opened the lid, Lenny and Thomas didn't see a tangle of Christmas lights, but instead found ropes and harnesses.

"What's that for?" Thomas asked. His dad had thrown so many curveballs their way on this trip, he figured anything was possible.

"We're going rock climbing at the Garden of the Gods," Dad replied.

"How do you rock climb in a garden?" Thomas asked.

"This place is nothing like your momma's vegetable patch," Dad said. "Your Nana and Pa took me there when I was twelve. I still remember it as if it were yesterday . . ."

Dad got a far off look in his eyes, the way he often did when he was reliving one of his favorite memories.

"What's with the name?" Thomas asked.

"Obviously, there's only one God," Dad replied, "but I guess it's fair to say this place is His garden. He owns everything. But if you're imagining tomato plants and corn stalks, think again. The park is full of some of the most amazing rock formations I've ever seen."

"I learned about that place in geography class," Lenny piped up. "The pictures look super cool!"

"Aw, son, the pictures aren't good enough. I honestly don't know how anyone could visit there and not know there is a God," Dad said.

Creation was one of Dad's favorite arguments for God's existence. Whether they were out fishing on a beautiful river, hiking a favorite trail, or just sitting outside under the stars, he'd often turn to his family and say, "Only a good God could create all of *this*."

Romans 1:20 says, "Ever since the world was created, people have seen the earth and sky. Through everything God made, they can clearly see his invisible qualities—his eternal power and divine nature. So they have no excuse for not knowing God."

You can understand a lot about God by paying attention to the world He has made. If possible, take this book outside. Look around for a moment. What can you learn about God by observing His creation? **Make a list below.**

_____

_____

_____

_____

_____

_____

_____

_____

They were just outside of Colorado Springs when their van started making a weird Thump! Thump! Thump!

Something wasn't right. The steering wheel started to shimmy. Dad said, "Whoa, girl," like he was still riding Fancy as he carefully maneuvered the van over to the side of the road.

"Stay put, guys," he said. He hopped out of the driver's seat to investigate.

The boys could hear the telltale sound of a tire going flat. HIIIIIISSSSSS!

"Well, that's just great," Lenny said.

Patience was not something he was good at, especially when plans changed unexpectedly. He crossed his arms and slid his baseball cap over his eyes. "Might as well take a snooze."

"I'm going to see if I can help," Thomas said, sliding out of his seat and stepping into the warm Colorado air. He came around the back of the van and saw his dad hunched down by the rear tire. Sweat was already pouring down Dad's beet-red face.

Dad was staring at the lug nuts of the wheel so hard it looked like he was trying to melt them with laser beam eyes. Apparently, he didn't hear the van door open or see Thomas in his peripheral vision because when Thomas said, "How can I help?" Dad nearly jumped out of his skin.

"Yikes, why'd ya sneak up on me like that, bud?" he said, as he wiped sweat from his face with the sleeve of his T-shirt.

"I didn't sneak up on you, Dad," Thomas replied, kicking at the roadside gravel with the toe of his sneaker. "I just thought maybe I could help."

He paused, expecting his dad's serious frown to turn into a grateful grin. It didn't. He just went back to staring at the lug nuts. "Can I grab the jack out of the back for you?" Thomas finally suggested, hoping to sweeten his dad's sour mood.

"That's the thing," Dad replied. "We don't have the jack. I set it aside when we were packing the luggage for this trip, and I just now realized that I never put it back. How am I going to change a tire without a jack?"

Thomas didn't answer. How *was* his dad supposed to change a flat tire without a jack?

Thomas went back and climbed into the back seat with his brother. "We gotta help Dad."

"Why? What's going on?" Lenny asked. While he wasn't always the most patient kid in the family, he often had good ideas.

"Well, the back tire is flat," Thomas explained, "and Dad just realized we don't have a jack."

"No jack? How could that happen?"

Though the boys were still several birthdays away from learning to drive, their dad had been teaching them the basics of car ownership and maintenance since they were young. They learned how to check the oil by age seven, how to help change a tire by age eight, and how to replace a spark plug by age nine. Their dad gave them frequent reminders that a responsible driver never leaves home without a tire jack.

Thomas shrugged his shoulders. "I dunno. He says he forgot it."

"I guess Dad was right," Lenny quipped. "Anything really can happen when you're out on the road." He paused a minute as the wheels inside his head began to turn.

Lenny started digging around in the back of the van trying to find something they could use to lift their vehicle high enough to allow Dad to slip off the flat tire.

Clank! Thump! Zip!

Lenny overturned all their belongings looking for something that would work. He was pretty good at science. His seventh grade science teacher was one of his favorites. She was always coming up with crazy experiments for them to try. She also taught him about gravitational force and how a simple fulcrum and lever could allow you to lift way more weight than if you just used your arms.

"Aha!" he finally said. "Thomas, come help me with this."

Lenny was pulling on the chrome handle of their dad's big metal toolbox. Just like he'd taught them never to leave home without a tire jack (oops!), their dad had also taught them to stash a set of tools in their vehicle on long road trips.

"It's heavy," Lenny said, leaning over the back seat. His brother was beside him, trying to get a good grip on the toolbox. "Let's lift it together. Ready? One. Two. Three!"

"This really *is* heavy," Thomas grunted, trying not to lose his grip.

"This will get the job done," Lenny replied.

"I don't get it," Thomas said, still huffing and puffing from the weight of the box.

"You will," Lenny replied.

Together, they got the toolbox out of the van, then they set it down in the grass to catch their breath for a moment. "Wait here," Lenny said.

"Where are you going?" Thomas asked, genuinely concerned. "Dad doesn't need us running off and causing him even more stress."

"I agree with your brother," Dad hollered over the car.

"I'm not running off," Lenny yelled back, already jogging away. "I saw exactly what we need just over there." He pointed to a small "Keep Colorado Clean" sign lying sideways in the grass off the side of the road.

"How's a damaged sign going to help?" Thomas shouted above the traffic noise coming from the busy highway.

"It's a lever!" Lenny said triumphantly. He knew his idea was a good one. He returned with a small green sign attached to a heavy-duty wooden post.

Though it was jagged at the bottom, the post was still about four feet long. The boys worked together to drag the toolbox and road sign over to their dad who looked hotter than ever and was clearly frustrated.

"I told you boys to stay in the car," he said.

"But Dad, I have an idea," Lenny said.

"Do I look like I want to hear one of your crazy ideas?" Dad asked.

The boys rarely saw this side of him. Their dad was typically cool as a cucumber. The heat and stress of the situation had drained him. Thomas started to retreat. He didn't want to add to his father's distress. Lenny was not so easily sidetracked.

"But Dad, this is a *really* good idea. We can use your toolbox as a fulcrum like this," he explained and slid the heavy box closer to the flat tire. "And the post from this old sign as a lever like this." He placed the post in the middle of the box and tipped it up like a teeter-totter.

"You're right. That is a good idea," Dad said as his face began to soften. "But it won't work."

"Why not?" Lenny asked. "We've got everything we need right here."

"You're right," Dad said as sweat oozed from every pore in his body, causing his shirt to stick to his chest, "but only in theory. There is no way that I can push down on the lever and slip off the old tire. It's a two-man job. Minimum."

"We'll have to work together," Lenny said.

"I can help!" Thomas added before fist-bumping his brother.

Dad did not share his sons' enthusiasm. "It's too dangerous," he said. "This is a busy road, and I can't keep my eye on you and on the tire."

"I'm twelve, Dad," Lenny said. "You don't have to babysit me every second. Plus, you're the one who is always telling us that there's nothing Team King can't conquer if we work together."

"Not happening," Dad said, wearing his grumpy face again. "I'm going to have to figure this one out all by myself."

Lenny looked at his brother. Thomas threw his hands in the air. They couldn't *force* their dad to let them help. Dejected, they walked around the front of the car and sat in the grass nearby. Lenny started bending stalks of weeds and popping the heads at his brother like tiny darts to pass the time. Thomas returned fire for a while until the heat and boredom took away his enthusiasm. Minutes melted together until more than an hour had passed.

"We're never gonna get out of here," Thomas said, groaning.

Just about the time they'd decided they might be sleeping on the side of the road, the boys heard their dad holler, "All right!"

"All right what?" Lenny asked his brother.

"All right, let's order pizza," Thomas joked.

"All right, we'll try your idea," Dad hollered.

Both boys were up and running quicker than you can say "peanut butter and jelly." (Try it! Can you say "peanut butter and jelly" in less time than "one-Mississippi"?)

"I'll work the lever," Lenny said, eager to help.

"I'll help Dad with the tire," Thomas said.

Once the end of the post was in place under the axle, Lenny moved to the other end of the post and pushed down with all his might. Their van raised off the ground just enough so that Dad and Thomas could unscrew the lug nuts and slide off the flat tire. Lenny lowered the lever as his dad rolled the spare tire around from the back of their vehicle. Then they repeated the process.

Lift. Slide. Tighten.

In no time at all, the new tire was secure.

"Good work, Team King," Dad said as he high-fived his boys.

His smile was back, and he seemed to toss his grumpies aside, along with the sign post.

"Dad, can you carry the toolbox back?" Lenny asked. "My biceps are sore!"

"Happy to," Dad said. His familiar smile once again stretched across his sweaty face. "But you're going to have to be a little tougher than that if you're going to make the basketball team next year."

"Maybe we should set up a toolbox and sign post in the backyard so I can do some reps when we get home," Lenny joked.

"Nah," Dad replied. "I'd rather not see that set up again any time soon."

"Shotgun!" Thomas declared, and before long they were back on the road and moving toward their next adventure.

Tag, You're It!

Whether you're naturally the life of the party or you prefer to spend your time alone absorbed in a project or book, **we all need other people.** Since the very first man (Adam) and the very first woman (Eve), humans have been created to build relationships with each other.

You've already read some of Genesis 2 and 3, but you may have missed the important words spoken by God and recorded in Genesis 2:18. According to this verse, what did God say was "not good"? **Write your answer below.**

_____

_____

_____

God's magnificent story, the Bible, begins with so much goodness:

- God created the light and called it "good" (Genesis 1:3–4).
- God created the oceans and called them "good" (Genesis 1:10).
- God created creatures to swarm, swim, and soar and called them "good" (Genesis 1:21).

Only one thing was "not good": God's beloved child facing the world alone.

You may be tempted to think that you don't need wise, Christian friends in order to live a life of faith, but, like the story you just read, **when we choose to face the challenges of life without the help of Jesus-loving friends, we make the journey much harder on ourselves.** In Ecclesiastes 4:9–10, God says, "Two people are better off than one, for they can help each other succeed. If one person falls, the other can reach out and help. But someone who falls alone is in real trouble."

"Real trouble." That's how the Bible describes someone who doesn't have wise, godly friends around him. You saw that play out in Dad's struggle with the flat tire. When he was determined to face the problem on his own, he was in *real trouble*. He was going to stay stuck on the side of the road in blistering heat forever. When he decided to lean on his sons, the problem was easily fixed. If you try to live a God-honoring life without the help of wise friends, you may find yourself stuck in the mud and mire with no one to pull you out.

Jesus is the best friend you'll ever have. He is always there for you, no matter what. But He has created you for connection with other people who can help you as you learn what it looks like to follow Him.

Most of the book of Proverbs was written by King Solomon to his son and the young people of Israel. King Solomon's words can help you grow in wisdom today. It is full of wisdom about friendship. **Look up each of the proverbs listed in the chart below, then write down the benefits of friendship the Bible promises.**

Verse	Benefits of Friendship
Proverbs 13:20	
Proverbs 17:17	
Proverbs 27:17	

Over the course of your life, you will have many friends. Some will share your interests; others will introduce you to something new. Some will be your age; others may be older or younger. Some may sit next to you in math class; others may live far away. Meaningful friendship can look a million different ways. What's most important for you to know is that you've been made for relationships with other people. Friends are one of God's greatest gifts to you. And while it's okay to be friends with

145

all different kinds of people, it's important that you surround yourself with friends who love Jesus and can help you grow to be more like Him. That way, when life gives you a flat tire, you have people who love you and love God to help you out.

Take a few minutes to reflect on your friendships. Make a list of your five closest friends. Brothers and cousins count. **Next to each name, write down how they help you grow in your relationship with Jesus.**

My Friends

_____

_____

_____

_____

_____

If you discover that you don't have many friends, or that most of your friends aren't following Jesus, take some time to talk to Jesus about that before moving on to the next chapter. Ask Him to give you friends who will help you grow in wisdom.

Jesus, thank You for being my best friend. I know that You are always there to help me when I need You. Bring friends into my life who will love me like You do and help me when I feel stuck. Teach me how to be a godly friend to others. Amen.

LIE #7:

"Following Jesus is boring."

TRUTH:

Following Jesus is a grand adventure!

If you'd asked Thomas a couple of weeks ago if he could head into an abandoned mine without his parents, he would have told you no. If you'd asked him if he could drive cattle on horseback, he might have laughed out loud. His fear of disappointing others had kept him from taking risks many times, but somehow, understanding God's grace and love had started to shift things inside of him. He didn't know how to rock climb. He wasn't sure if he would succeed or fail, but he had a new confidence that came from knowing that his acceptance wasn't based on always being good and never making a mistake.

Now at the base of a mountain, his confidence felt shaky. "Are we gonna climb *those*?" he asked, staring up at the towering red rock formations of Garden of the Gods.

Though they were close enough to reach out and touch, the rocks' position under the indigo Colorado sky made them look like a painting.

"We won't start there, mate," said their climbing guide, Alex.

He had a laid-back personality, he looked like a surfer, and he sported the accent of his homeland, Australia. "I bet your dad could tackle that slope pretty easily, though," he said, tossing a carabiner to Lenny.

Dad was currently struggling to put on his bright blue climbing helmet. He smiled at Alex's suggestion.

"I'm game if you're game," he said.

Thomas got the feeling that Dad and Alex were telling a joke and that he didn't understand the punchline.

Alex was their personal guide for the day. He taught them the basics like how to "tie in" using a figure eight knot, how to communicate with each other during a climb using phrases like "belay on" and "climb on," and how to spot a good hold in the rock face to grab with their hands or feet. Though they spent a lot of time in the learning phase, it didn't feel like school. Alex's enthusiasm for climbing was infectious, and they soaked in the new information like kitchen sponges.

As the sun began to glare at them from its highest point in the sky, Alex said they were ready. "Time to head to the Snake Pit," he announced.

"Cool!" Lenny declared. "I *love* snakes!"

"Good on you, mate," Alex said, "but I doubt you'll see any actual snakes there. That's just the name locals give to the area where *you're* going to become a rock climber. Let's see how you do with the Mighty Mongoose!"

The Mighty Mongoose was a 15-foot boulder with plenty of good holds for hands and feet. With constant coaching from Alex, Lenny was up the big rock in no time. He rappelled down with a huge smile on his face.

"That was awesome!" he shouted. "Let's do something bigger!"

He'd have to wait until his brother and dad had their turns wrestling the Mongoose. Thomas was a natural. Less expressive than his older brother, he quietly concentrated on each move and climbed up the boulder with precision. He rappelled down in four smooth kicks before high-fiving his dad on the ground.

"You make it look easy, son," Dad said, beaming.

The boys expected their dad to struggle on his first trek up a boulder, but he quickly proved them wrong. He seemed to know exactly what to do and where all the good holds were without having to search for them. He made it to the top quicker than either of them had. He was back on the ground with two smooth kicks and the boys realized, to their amazement, that he hadn't even broken a sweat.

"Why are you so good at this?" Lenny asked suspiciously. He didn't say it out loud, but he was secretly hoping to be the best of the bunch. "That looked like you've been climbing for years."

"I have," Dad said, with a shrug and a smile.

"No way!" Thomas replied. "I've *never* seen you rock climb or even heard you talk about it."

"There's a lot about your old dad you don't know, bud," Dad said, pulling Thomas in for a side hug. "Where did you think that tub of climbing gear came from?"

"Walmart?" Thomas guessed.

That made Dad laugh.

"I'm afraid they don't sell that gear at Walmart," Dad said. "All of that stuff is from my days as a competitive climber. Your momma used to compete too. She's a rockstar of a rock climber. When we get home, you should ask her to show you some of her awards."

Lenny and Thomas looked at their dad. Then they looked at each other, then back at their dad again.

"Rock star and rock climber," Lenny finally said. "Those are four words I never thought I'd hear to describe my mom."

He tried to picture her. She was probably putting Lucy down for a nap or lying on the floor playing cars with their little brother, Mikey. He tried to imagine her hanging from the side of a mountain, but the image wouldn't come.

climbing Together '98

"You've got to be pulling my leg," he said.

"No leg pulling here, boys," Dad replied. "Alex and I met at a climbing competition many moons ago."

"True story," Alex said as he worked to wind their climbing ropes into neat coils.

Lenny shook his head. Thomas tried to scratch his before remembering he was still wearing a helmet. They could not believe what they were hearing! Over the course of a few days, their dad had transformed in their minds from an ordinary man to a superhero! He could ride horses, rope cows, and now, they learned, climb mountains!

"I believe you're ready for White Spire," Alex announced, tossing a rope to Lenny. "Now the adventure *really* begins."

Alex led the team to a pair of tall boulders known as The Twins made up of two humongous rock towers, one white and one red.

"There she is," Alex said with admiration in his voice. With a flick of his chin he nodded to the white twin. "Fifty feet of adventure, just waiting for you."

By now both boys realized that the butterflies in their stomachs and sweat on their palms was part of the experience. Luckily, excitement overrode their nervousness. They buckled their helmet straps and prepared to face the mountain. This time Dad went first.

"On belay," Dad said.

"Belay on," Alex called.

"Climbing," Dad said.

"Climb on," Alex echoed back.

"Did I mention that I climbed this with Pa when I was around your age?" Dad asked as he found his first handhold.

"Pa is a rock climber too?" Thomas asked. "It's like my family is made up of secret agents," he muttered, as he watched a blue butterfly flutter near his dad's head.

"Well, I don't know if he would *still* call himself a rock climber," Dad said, as he moved higher up the rock face. "But back in the day, your Pa was always up for an adventure, especially one with his boy."

Again, Lenny tried to picture the story as Dad described it. Pa as an eager rock climber? He thought of his grandpa sitting in his big recliner watching football on the big screen. He liked the thought of him being younger and willing to try anything.

Dad as a little boy? That one was a little easier to imagine. Everyone had always told Lenny that he looked just like his dad. So, he imagined himself on the mountain, smiling from ear to ear.

Learn to Tie a Climbing Knot

Every rock climber knows how to tie a figure eight, a basic knot that allows you to "tie in" before you climb.

Step 1: Make a loop in your rope, about two feet from the end.

Step 2: Hold the loop in place, and wrap the rope once around the base of the loop.

Step 3: Insert the end of the rope through the loop.

Step 4: Pull both ends of the rope to reveal a figure eight.

Step 5: Trace the figure eight knot with the end of the rope, starting at the bottom to make a double figure eight.

. . .

The foursome spent the rest of the day climbing the White Spire together. Halfway up, Thomas had a moment when he felt like he couldn't go on. His muscles felt too tired. The next hold felt *just* out of reach. "I can't do it!" he yelled down toward the ground.

Lenny often gave his brother a hard time, but deep down, he wanted to see Thomas succeed. He said a quick prayer before responding, "I'm praying for you. I know you can do it." Alex patted Lenny on the shoulder before yelling up to Thomas: "Breathe. Pray. Trust."

For Thomas, this was a moment he would look back on as the time he learned he could turn to Jesus whenever he needed to. With his brother cheering him on, Thomas reached the summit. On the top of the White Spire, he took a moment to survey God's creation. What he saw was hard to put into words: huge boulders, a never-ending sky, birds and insects that seemed as free as he felt right then. Yes, God was real, and He was good. Thomas rappelled down to celebratory hugs and high fives.

As the day ended and the sun dipped below the horizon, turning the blue sky into a panorama of pink and orange, the crew sat together with their backs against the rock they had conquered, munching on trail mix and drinking cold water from their metal flasks. Working as a team was essential to their success that day. They couldn't have done it on their own—*and they wouldn't have wanted to.* Though each of them ultimately conquered the rock, they also experienced moments of frustration, fear, and self-doubt on their way to the top. Their muscles ached. Still, a sense of accomplishment wrapped each boy like a warm blanket. They'd done it! They'd learned a new skill, faced their fears, and accomplished the goal. For a long time, they sat in silence, enjoying the breathtaking scenery.

"I don't ever want this feeling to go away," Thomas finally said, piercing the silence, just as the crickets and katydids began their evening concert.

"What feeling?" Dad asked.

"This feeling of adventure. I miss Momma and my friends, but normal life just seems so boring compared to this. I mean, it's going to be pretty hard to go back to doing chores after becoming a treasure-hunting, cattle-driving, slingshot-wielding rock climber."

"Ughhh, math homework!" Lenny groaned as he realized the realities of what awaited him at home. "I hate math homework!" he added, as if anyone had any doubts.

"*Life* is the big adventure, mate," Alex assured them.

"Easy for you to say," Lenny replied. "You climb mountains for a living."

"Fair point," Alex conceded. "Do you want to know what I was doing with my life before I decided to become a follower of Jesus?"

"Sure!" Lenny said.

"This is a good story," Dad chimed in.

"I'll tell them the short version," Alex said, giving Dad an elbow nudge to the ribs. "The short answer is . . . *nothing.* I was living for myself, constantly trying to find what would make me happy: music, girlfriends, vacations, different jobs. I tried all kinds of things. Not all of them were bad for me, but none of them could give me peace, at least not for very long.

"I was introduced to Jesus through a ministry to rock climbers that your mum and dad were a part of. Rock climbing had always been a hobby of mine, something I did for myself, to look fit and impress other people."

"Don't you mean to impress girls?" Dad asked, returning Alex's elbow jab.

"Hey! Girls are people!" Alex joked.

"But when I became a Christian, that's when the real adventure began. I didn't just want to live for my own happiness. I wanted my life to bring God glory. No one is more surprised than me that He took a hobby—rock climbing—and turned it into a way for me to help young men like you follow Jesus too."

"Alex now leads the climbing ministry we used to serve with," Dad said proudly. "Every year he helps more than two hundred young men learn to climb as a way to share Christ with them."

"See?" Alex said. "What an adventure!"

"I'm loving this conversation," Dad said. "But this old man needs a real dinner. No offense to your trail mix, friend," he said to Alex.

"Help your dad up," Dad said to Thomas. Thomas grabbed his dad's hands and pulled him up with a grunt. The soreness in their muscles was really setting in.

"That means you get to lift this old man," Alex said to Lenny. "I can still outclimb most anybody," he added, "but I need to soak longer and longer in a hot bath afterward."

"You're coming to the campsite for dinner, aren't you, Alex?" Dad asked. "I'm making my world-famous cast-iron pizza."

"Not tonight," Alex said, squeezing his old friend's shoulder. "I've got a group of ten climbing tomorrow, and I need to sort their gear. They aren't as handsome as you fellas, but they smell better, so it's a tradeoff," he joked.

"I never leave the trailhead without thanking God for giving us a good climb," he then announced. "One of you boys want to pray?"

Though his mouth felt dry, and his stomach tightened a little, Thomas decided to volunteer.

"Jesus," he began, "thank You for making this place. Thank You for letting me come here. Thank You for keeping us safe today. Help Alex to be safe as he leads the climb tomorrow. Help those boys to see who You are just like I did today."

Then he added, "Oh and, thank You for campfire pizza. Amen."

"Amen!" the rest of the crew said at once.

"Let's eat!" Lenny added as they grabbed their gear and headed back the way they'd come.

Tag, You're it!

Be honest, does following Jesus ever seem a little *boring* to you? When you think of what it means to be a Christian, do you picture things like going to church, singing old songs, or trying to read really hard words in the Bible?

Think again. The Bible is filled with stories of great adventures, dramatic journeys, and good guy vs. bad guy battles:

- God called Noah to the biggest boat ride of all time (Genesis 6:14–15).
- He told Moses to take on the most powerful bad guy in the world with nothing more than a wooden staff in his hand (Exodus 3).
- He called the Israelites to leave their home in Egypt and travel to a place they'd never seen (Exodus 6:6–8). They didn't have GPS or even maps back then. They were totally dependent on God to show them the way.
- God helped David face a trash-talking giant with nothing more than a slingshot (1 Samuel 17).
- He called fishermen to leave their familiar nets and help Him turn the world upside down (more about that in a minute).

Talk about adventures! Your craving for adventure is not an accident; God made you that way. These are the words He used in His Word to describe godly men:

- Strong
- Self-controlled
- Respectable
- Wise
- Courageous

Not:

- Weak
- Boring
- Predictable

To live for Jesus means to deny yourself and to follow Him wherever He leads. He often leads His children to exciting and even dangerous places they would never have chosen for themselves. Sometimes that means being a missionary in a faraway country where people haven't heard about Jesus' love. Sometimes it means getting over your fear and talking to the kid who sits alone at lunch. Sometimes the adventures are big and everyone knows about them. Sometimes it is a simple step of obedience done without any human praise.

The apostle Paul knew a thing or two about the adventurous Christian life. Listen to how he described it:

> I have worked harder, been put in prison more often, been whipped times without number, and faced death again and again. . . . Three times I was beaten with rods. Once I was stoned. Three times I was shipwrecked. Once I spent a whole night and a day adrift at sea. I have traveled on many long journeys. I have faced danger from rivers and from robbers. . . . I have faced danger in the cities, in the deserts, and on the seas. (2 Corinthians 11:23–26)

Go back and read that passage again. This time, circle some of the adventures Paul experienced because he was a follower of Jesus.

You may never face a shipwreck or a day adrift at sea. God may not ask you to go to prison or be whipped for His name's sake, but He has called you to live a life that looks different from the lives of those who don't know Christ. And He has promised an eternal future for you that is more amazing than you could ever imagine (1 Corinthians 2:9). Good news! Cloud-sitting and harp concerts are never part of the picture of heaven you might have imagined. It's a lot more amazing than that. **Following Jesus is never boring. It is the grand adventure!**

. . .

Lenny and Thomas finished setting up the tent just as Dad announced, "Pizza's ready!" They each plopped into a camp chair as he handed them paper plates nearly collapsing under big wood-fired pizza slices covered in ooey-gooey cheese and crispy pepperoni. As they impatiently waited for their food to cool, Dad pulled three soda bottles from a small cooler nearby.

"I asked Alex to sneak these into the van for me," Dad said, prying the metal caps off the two bottles before handing them to his boys.

TRUSTIES ROOT BEER

The bottles had "Trusties" printed in orange ink across the front.

"This root beer is made right here in Colorado. None of that fake sugar stuff in these. This root beer is made the old-fashioned way with real cane sugar. I enjoyed one of these for the first time on that trip I took with your Nana and Pa as a boy. I've craved it ever since. I love it so much that your mom even surprised me by having a case shipped in for our wedding."

"Another amazing story you've never told us, Dad," Thomas said.

"Yum!" Lenny gulped his bottle down, letting some roll down his chin. Then he let out a big *"BEEELLLCH!"* before pounding his chest.

"Excuse you!" Thomas said.

Lenny replied with a smile and a smaller *"Burrrp!"*

Thomas took a sip, then set his soda aside, trying to calculate how he could get one drink in with every single bite of pizza.

Like so many other nights on this trip, the day ended with a campfire and a Bible story. The boys had kept up with their Bible reading like they'd promised Pastor Ralph (for the most part). Lenny was almost all the way through the book of John.

Thomas was moving more slowly, taking the time to imagine what each of the stories of Jesus' time on earth would have been like.

"Quiz time!" Dad said. "Do you remember the names of some of Jesus' first disciples? You read about them in the first chapter of John."

Thomas had to think about it. Lenny knew the answer but struggled to speak with a mouth full of campfire pizza. It came out like, "Andwewww!"

"Andrew!" Thomas said, catching on quickly.

"Hey! Ayyy gotitfirst," Lenny mumbled around a mouth full of cheese.

"Fortunately for you, Lenny, I speak pizza," Dad said. "Right. Andrew was one of them. Who else?"

"Simon!" Lenny said, forcing himself to swallow first. "And Philip," he added.

"I'm impressed," Dad said, putting on a headlamp and pulling his Bible from a nearby backpack. "Here's a tougher one. What did those disciples do for a living?"

Thomas looked at Lenny, expecting him to know the answer.

"Don't look at me," Lenny said. "You got any more of those root beers, Dad?" he asked before stuffing his mouth full of another bite of pizza.

"Check the cooler," Dad replied. "It was a bit of a trick question. The book of John doesn't list their jobs, but the book of Matthew does. Sometimes the writers of the Bible told the same story more than once and shared different details."

Dad adjusted his headlamp so that he could read from his Bible. Lenny put on his own headlamp. Thomas clicked on a flashlight and pointed it at his brother.

"Matthew 4:18 says, 'One day as Jesus was walking along the shore of the Sea of Galilee, he saw two brothers—Simon, also called Peter, and Andrew—throwing a net into the water, for they fished for a living.'"

"Fishermen, huh?" Thomas said. "I knew I liked those guys."

"I've been thinking about what you said, Thomas, about not wanting the adventure to end," Dad said, also munching on his own slice of pizza. "I should have done a better job of telling you about the many adventures God has taken me on. And I'm not just talking about the things you've discovered on this trip."

"Like the fact that you used to rock climb?" Lenny asked.

"Or that Momma did?" Thomas added.

"I've always wanted you to feel safe and stable," Dad said, setting his empty paper plate on the ground. "I *still* want you to feel safe and stable, but you're getting older now and I also want you to see how amazing living for Jesus really is.

"Marrying your momma has been an adventure. Having you guys and your brother and sister join our family has been an adventure. Pastoring a church is an adventure. . . . Sometimes it feels like a fight between good and evil, to be honest.

"God is in charge, and that can be exciting and scary and fun and uncomfortable all at the same time. But I can tell you one thing, it is *never* boring. When I read my Bible and look around at the amazing world He created, it seems obvious to me that God isn't boring and that He doesn't ask us to live a boring life either."

"But, Dad," Thomas said, "sometimes life *is* boring. Like when Momma makes me clean my room or—no offense—when the sermon at church goes on too long."

"No offense taken, my boy," Dad said with a laugh. "I want to get to lunch after church just as much as you do.

"I'm not saying you'll never have a dull moment. I just want you to know that following Jesus is the greatest adventure you will ever be on. So, you don't have to worry that all the fun is going to end just because we'll be heading home soon."

Dad stood up and stretched before downing the rest of his root beer. "I've loved every minute of this trip with you boys," Dad assured them, "but this dad bod is ready to sleep in a real bed. I miss your momma and your little brother and sister. Tomorrow, we point ourselves toward home."

"You going to eat those?" Thomas asked, pointing to a pile of pizza crusts on his brother's plate.

"Go for it," Lenny replied. He slid the crusts onto his brother's plate before tossing his own into the campfire. He stood there watching the plate burst into flames as Thomas crunch, crunch, crunched beside him.

Lenny plopped back down onto his camp chair and thrust his arms upward to stretch his back. Rock climbing left his muscles tired and sore.

"Before we hit the hay, I've got one more quiz for you," Dad said. "Whoever gets this right gets unlimited Trusties on the ride home."

That perked the boys up!

"How would the disciples have spent their lives if they'd never met Jesus?"

Silence. Both boys were thinking.

"Fishing?" Thomas said.

"Yep, fishing. I know you love to fish, and so do I, but instead, the disciples chose to go to the ends of the earth telling people about Jesus."

"Did I win the Trusties?" Thomas asked.

"We'll talk about it tomorrow," Dad replied, yawning.

The tired climbers zipped into their tent and shimmied into their sleeping bags. It was a day made of memories they'd never forget, but the real adventure had just begun.

Tag, You're It!

When Jesus invited the first disciples to be a part of His work in the world, He gave them a simple command, "Come, follow me" (John 1:43). Notice what He *didn't* say:

- "Being My follower will always be easy."
- "Your life will always go exactly the way you've planned."
- "Following Me will never cost you anything."

He just said, "Come, follow me." In many ways, the disciples were taking a leap without a safety net. What greater adventure exists?

There is no guarantee that following Jesus will mean nonstop thrills. There will be highs and lows and many moments of ordinary obedience. Still, a life lived for Jesus is a trade up from a life lived for yourself. As you grow and mature in your faith, knowing God through His Word and living for Him will be an epic adventure. Every day is a new opportunity to trust Him. *He* is your safety net!

You may not be sitting in a fishing boat as you read these words, but your life is not all that different from the early disciples. Jesus is saying to you: "Come, follow me." You don't know where He will take you. You can't see what obstacles you might face along the way. But you can know for sure that Jesus is worth following.

Will you join the Grand Adventure and go wherever He asks you to go?

Write Jesus a note telling Him that you will follow Him anywhere. If you still feel unsure or a little scared, tell Him that too, and ask Him to help you trust that He has amazing plans for your life.

Dear Jesus,

_____
(Your signature)

LIE #8:
"I can't control myself."

TRUTH:
You have a Helper.

Dad woke the boys up just as the first streaks of sunlight became visible on the horizon. The time had come for them to head back home, and he wanted to get an early start. Still groggy from a short night spent sleeping on the ground, and a little sad to see the adventure end, Lenny and Thomas packed up the tent in silence as their dad loaded the camp chairs, put out the fire, and checked the pressure on all four tires.

The sun began its slow ascent as they jumped into their road-trip-mobile and headed east. Lenny was too sleepy to call, "Shotgun!" but he still protested when his brother slid into the front seat. "You rode shotgun last time!"

"That doesn't mean *you* get it," Thomas shot back. Lenny stretched his seat belt out to lean forward and try to give his brother a wet willy.

Thomas swung his elbow backward in protest.

"Ouch!" Lenny yelled, before slapping the top of his little brother's head.

Screeech! Dad slammed on the brakes. Both boys lunged forward against their seat belts.

"That's enough!" Dad said sternly. "We've got a long drive ahead of us, and I'm not going to spend it listening to you two fight about who gets to sit where."

"He started it," Thomas whined.

"Did not," Lenny argued.

"All right," Dad said, clearly exasperated. "Both of you in the back. I don't want to hear another peep until somebody spots a road sign for Kansas."

"But Daaad," the brothers complained in unison.

"Zip it!" Dad said. "We are not going to spoil this amazing trip by spending the last few hours whining and fighting. Understood?"

"Understood," Lenny muttered.

"Yes, sir," Thomas said, taking one more swat at his brother.

The miles passed slowly as silence filled the car like helium in a balloon. Lenny curled up in his seat and fell fast asleep. In no time at all, he was back climbing the White Spire in his dreams.

Thomas, on the other hand, crossed his arms and stared out the window as a million angry thoughts flooded his brain:

Why does Lenny always think he deserves to sit in the front?
He started it.
I'm tired of him pushing me around . . .

He tried to pray that God would help him let go of his anger toward his brother, but his frustrations seemed to choke out the words. Though he'd had the time of his life on this trip, including many amazing memories with his big brother, right now, he was seeing red. He couldn't seem to stop the anger from welling up inside of him again and again like waves crashing onto the beach.

Memories of moments when his brother treated him unfairly streamed through his mind like clips from a movie:

He insisted on going first up the Mongoose . . . he always makes
me go last.

He ate the last toaster pastry this morning. Typical.

He always takes the easy chores and leaves the hard work for me.

Thomas remembered battling this same anger on the cattle drive. He didn't want to feel so annoyed, but, he reasoned, "I can't help myself," and "If Lenny didn't act that way, I wouldn't feel this way."

Thomas was still lost in his frustrations when his brother popped his head up and announced, "I saw the Kansas sign first! Take that, loser!" he said, pointing his finger at his brother.

Without a second thought, Thomas unclicked his seat belt and tackled Lenny.

"You are such a jerk!" he yelled, punching his brother in the chest. "You think you're better than me. YOU AREN'T BETTER THAN ME!" he screamed.

In a flash, Dad pulled the car to the side of the road and jolted to a stop. This time it wasn't to fix a flat tire but to try to settle the emotional tsunami happening in the back seat.

In a series of swift moves, Dad threw the car into park, jumped out of his seat, opened the back door, and grabbed his younger son by the T-shirt.

"That's enough," he said.

"Get him off of me!" Lenny shouted.

Thomas kept hitting. The fuse of his temper had been lit, and it felt like dynamite was exploding inside of him.

"I said that's enough!" Dad repeated, wedging his body between his two sons.

"Let's take a walk," he said to Thomas. "Lenny, stay in the car."

"Why am *I* in trouble?" Lenny asked.

"Give us some space," Dad responded, looking Lenny in the eye.

"Got it," Lenny said. He knew when his dad meant business.

Dad and Thomas walked along the emergency lane on the right side of the highway for about fifty yards, then, following Dad's lead, they turned around and walked back to the car. They completed that loop four or five times in silence while Thomas's internal thermometer cooled off.

Finally, Dad said, "We need to talk about what happened back there, son."

Thomas kicked at a rock. He didn't want to talk about it. Regret had already wrapped itself around his mind and heart.

Why did I act like that? he wondered. *Lenny is my best friend; why did I get so angry?*

The last few minutes felt like a needle had popped the balloon of the happy trip. All the happy memories and good feelings seemed to be leaking out of him as he stood on the side of the road watching cars whiz by.

He was mad at himself for getting so mad. In many ways, he was so disciplined. He worked hard at school, practiced diligently for sports, and kept his room clean. But, when it came to his anger, he often felt like the Incredible Hulk, unable to control his feelings or the damage they caused.

Dad just stood there staring at him. He obviously wasn't going to let Thomas off the hook.

"I dunno, Dad," Thomas finally said, unable to look his dad in the eye. "Sometimes I get so angry, I just can't control myself."

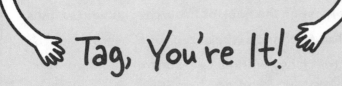

Tag, You're It!

Is there something in your life that makes you feel out of control? Like Thomas, it might be your anger. Or perhaps you struggle with lying or jealousy.

It can be tempting to throw up your hands and decide that the downward pull of something is just too strong. When you've tried and failed to make a change, it's easy to think, "I can't have self-control in the area of _____."

Ask God to show you any areas of your life where you lack self-control. Circle those areas in the group of words below.

Arguing with Parents   Temper   Caring for Belongings

Words   Habits   Bedtime   Way I Treat Others

Way I Treat My Parents   Personal Hygiene   Shows I Watch

Screen Time   Obeying Authorities   Foods I Eat

Sites I Visit on the Internet

The Truth is, because we are sinners, everyone struggles with self-control and **the Bible makes it clear that our lack of self-control can put us in a dangerous position.**

Remember how most of the book of Proverbs was written by a dad to his son? King Solomon (the author of Proverbs) wanted his son to know that living without self-control would put his boy in harm's way. Proverbs 25:28 says,

> A person without self-control
>   is like a city with broken-down walls.

What do you think Solomon meant by that? Write your answer below.

_____

_____

_____

Remember: Satan is a liar. His goal is to deceive you into believing lies about God, yourself, and others. Lacking self-control makes you vulnerable to his attacks because you are being driven by your feelings instead of the Truth. Self-control works like a strong, fortified wall, protecting you from the missiles of deceit he wants to shoot at you.

But what can you do when you've tried to have self-control? You don't *want* to yell at your mom . . . the candy in the pantry seems to be calling your name . . . you find yourself sneaking to watch something that you know you shouldn't watch. . . . What do you do when self-control feels impossible? Run to your Helper!

Read the two passages below. In each one, underline the words "self-control." Draw an arrow to where self-control comes from.

"For God gave us a spirit not of fear but of power and love and self-control." (2 Timothy 1:7 ESV)

"But the Holy Spirit produces this kind of fruit in our lives: love, joy, peace, patience, kindness, goodness, faithfulness, gentleness, and self-control." (Galatians 5:22–23)

The term "self-control" may make it sound like God expects you to handle things all on your own, but there are many habits and patterns we cannot break by ourselves. God knows that! He has given us self-control as a gift. **What you need most is not self-control, it's Spirit-control!** The Holy Spirit will help you win the battle against your struggle with sin and teach you how to make choices that will please God.

Self-control is the wall that protects you from the lies of the enemy. When you find yourself struggling to make the right choice or to turn away from something that you know is bad for you, pray to Jesus! Ask Him to help you and to protect you from decisions that will hurt you.

Let's practice! You don't need any fancy words. Just pray something like, "Jesus, I struggle to have self-control in the area of _____. I know that isn't good for me. Holy Spirit, please help me."

. . .

Tears of rage had transformed to tears of regret. Thomas felt bad for losing his temper, disobeying his dad, and hitting his brother. He also knew that he had sinned. He wanted to do better, but deep down, he knew he couldn't do that on his own.

"You're right, Thomas," Dad said. "You can't always control yourself, at least not on your own. Neither can I and neither can your brother. Remember what you learned on the cattle drive? God doesn't love you because you never make mistakes. He loves you because you're His child. What can you do when you've blown it?"

"Ask God to forgive me," Thomas replied sheepishly.

"That's right," Dad said, "and will He?"

"I guess so," Thomas said, still feeling squashed by the weight of his mistakes.

"You guess so?" Dad asked, pulling his son in for a hug.

"I know so," Thomas replied. "It's hard to believe, but I know Jesus will forgive me when I ask Him to."

"Isn't that good news?!" Dad asked, pulling back and looking down at Thomas. "And here's the icing on the cake. He won't just forgive you. He has given you the Holy Spirit to help you have more self-control next time."

"Dad?" Thomas asked. "Do you ever struggle with self-control?"

"May I remind you of the tire temper tantrum I threw just a few days ago?" Dad said, tousling his son's hair.

"Oh, yeah," Thomas replied. "I forgot about that already."

"So has God," Dad said. "And boy am I glad! Nobody's perfect, son. That's why we need Jesus so much. It's also why He has given us the gift of His Spirit to help us grow more like Him. Don't make up your mind that you can never win the battle against your temper. Jesus will help you if you ask Him to."

"But," Thomas said, as worry crept back into his mind like a slow-moving spider. "What if I mess up again?"

"You will," Dad said matter-of-factly. "I will. Your brother will. We all need grace by the dump truck load. But Jesus is working inside of us, making us more like Him every day."

They walked back to the van side by side. Lenny was standing at the front of the van waiting for them.

"I'm sorry I always take the front seat," Lenny said to his brother. "I know that probably makes you feel like I don't care about what you want."

"It's okay," Thomas said. He was trying to work up the nerve to apologize to his brother. He didn't expect to hear Lenny apologize first.

"And I'm sorry I called you a loser," Lenny added. "I wish I hadn't said that."

"I forgive you," Thomas said. "I'm sorry I got so angry and hit you."

"Don't forget the part about calling me a jerk," Lenny teased.

"I'm sorry I called you a jerk," Thomas said, trying not to smile.

The brothers were buds once again.

Dad put a hand on each boy's shoulder. "I'm going to say this one more time," he said. "Our trip is almost over. We are not going to spend it fighting like two spider monkeys at the zoo. Got it?"

"Got it," Lenny said.

"Got it," Thomas nodded.

"Why don't you take shotgun?" Lenny asked his brother.

"Then you can have it at the next stop," Thomas offered.

The brothers fist-bumped, and Team King was on the road again.

Tag, You're It!

Have you ever heard the phrase "pull yourself up by your bootstraps"? Try to picture Hank the cowboy getting ready for another cattle drive. The last step he'd take before heading out the door would be to pull on his boots. Most boots have a little loop on the side or the back that is meant to help slide the boot on. But can you imagine trying to lift yourself up in the air with that loop while you have them on? That's the image of "pulling yourself up by your bootstraps." Impossible. It's also a saying that means doing something without any help.

Following Jesus was never meant to be a pull-yourself-up-by-your-bootstraps kind of life. **You don't have to figure it all out on your own or impress Jesus by always trying harder. He wants you to depend on Him every day.**

Did you know that your parents want you to ask them for help? It's true! They want you to feel safe enough to always come to them when a problem is too big for you to solve on your own. **Your heavenly Father feels the same way!**

Jesus said, "Come to me, all of you who are weary and carry heavy burdens, and I will give you rest" (Matthew 11:28). Did you hear what He said?

Come to me!

When your emotions feel out of control: come to Jesus!
When you are tempted to sin: come to Jesus!
When you can't control your cravings: come to Jesus!
When you've sinned: come to Jesus!
When life feels out of control: come to Jesus!
When you've tried and failed to make a change: come to Jesus!

Being a Christian isn't about muscling up or trying harder. It's about admitting you can't do it on your own, turning to Jesus every day, and saying, "I need your help today!"

- He has given you His Word to guide you.
- He has given you a family to love you.
- He has given you wise friends to help you when you're stuck.
- He has given you the Holy Spirit to give you Spirit-control when you lack self-control.

The next time you feel like you just can't do the right thing, run to Jesus and ask the Holy Spirit to help—no bootstraps necessary!

LIE #9:
"I'm too young to ________"
TRUTH:
You are who you're becoming.

Oh, I can't wait to get home, home, home . . ." For miles, Dad had been singing the silly song he made up. Though it meant they'd get home well after midnight, his plan was to drive straight through without stopping for the night.

"I'm ready to see your momma!" Dad declared as they crossed the border into their home state.

"I'm ready to sleep in my own bed," Lenny announced.

"I'm ready to check on Earl!" Thomas added. Earl was his pet lizard, a yellow leopard gecko with black spots. "I bet he's hungry!"

"I'm sure you're right," Dad agreed. "When I give the sermon at church tomorrow, do you think I should tell them that I hold the fastest rock climbing record?"

"They won't believe you!" Lenny joked.

"I'll have to show them the pictures to prove it," Dad said. "What a great trip." He let out a deep sigh and kept his eye on the road. "One last road trip meal, dudes! What should we have?"

"Pizza!" Thomas said.

"Wings," Lenny added.

"How about tacos?" Dad asked, pointing at a sign ahead for Taco Willy's. "According to their billboard, Taco Willy's has the best tacos along Route 66."

"Only one way to find out!" Lenny said.

Taco Willy's was a tiny, metal building surrounded by colorful picnic tables. String lights hung above the eating area and mariachi music played through an old, crackly speaker.

"What can I get you fellas?" A waitress with bright green glasses and blonde hair pulled a pen from behind her ear to take their order.

"What's good?" Dad asked. (Dads always ask questions like that.)

"Honey, it's *all* good," she replied. "We have tacos and nachos, take your pick."

"Tacos for me," Dad said.

"Nachos!" Thomas said.

"Can I get both?" Lenny asked.

"Why not?" Dad replied. Vacation Dad sure was fun.

A few minutes later, the waitress delivered red plastic baskets loaded with tacos and nachos. Cheese, sour cream, salsa, black beans, jalapeños . . . they could barely find the chips and shells that were buried underneath mountains of toppings.

"Do I look different?" Lenny asked as he picked up a chip covered in cheese and sour cream.

"What do you mean?" Dad asked, taking a huge bite of taco. A stream of salsa began to run down his chin.

"I *feel* different," Lenny said. "I learned so much on this trip about our family, about myself, and about God. It seems a little strange to think about going back to my life before."

"I'm glad," Dad said. "I wanted this to be the trip of a lifetime. But you know," he added, munching on his third taco, "now is the perfect time to make changes to become the man you want to be. My grandpa always used to say, 'You are who you're becoming.'"

"That's confusing," Thomas said as he flicked a jalapeño from the top of his nacho mountain.

"What he meant was that who you are in the future will look a lot like who you are now," Dad clarified.

"Did you forget that I'm only in middle school?" Lenny asked. "It's a little early to start planning my future, don't you think?"

"What's in this?" Dad asked, picking up a bottle of salsa that was sitting on the table.

"Salsa?" Thomas answered, thinking maybe it was a trick question.

"That's right, salsa," Dad said. "And what's salsa made out of?"

"Tomatoes?" Thomas replied, still thinking the questions were too easy.

"What kind of seed do you plant to grow a tomato?" Dad asked.

"A tomato seed?" Thomas said.

"That's right!" Dad said. "And to grow corn, you plant a corn seed. To grow carrots, you plant a carrot seed. To grow watermelon, you plant a watermelon seed."

"We get the idea, Dad," Lenny said.

"Well, the same is true for our lives. Some people might say that you're too young to hunt treasure, but you did it! Some might think that you're too young to be real cowboys, but you did that too."

"And we went rock climbing!" Lenny said.

"And changed a tire!" Thomas added.

"You're capable of doing so many things," Dad said, "and the kind of man you become will be determined by the way you spend your time *right now*. You don't just turn eighteen and flip a magic switch to become wise.

"You learned how to plant some new seeds on this trip: reading your Bible daily, resting in God's forgiveness, depending on Him for self-control. If you keep watering those seeds, you are going to grow up to be amazing, godly men."

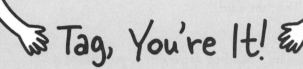

Tag, You're It!

Close your eyes and try to picture yourself ten or fifteen years from now.

- What kind of job will you have?
- Is there a hobby or skill you hope to master by then?
- Will you have a family of your own? What kind of dad and husband do you want to be?
- Will you have grown in your walk with Jesus? What will that look like?

The Bible says, "Don't be misled—you cannot mock the justice of God. **You will always harvest what you plant**" (Galatians 6:7).

That means that if you want to become a great basketball player, you need to spend a lot of time practicing free throws and lay-ups. If you want to be an amazing musician, you must invest many hours practicing. And **if you want to grow up to be a wise man who loves God's Word and shares the gospel with others, you must plant those seeds now and water them at every stage of your life.**

In contrast, if you spend most of your time playing video games, scrolling social media, or watching TV, the "fruit" that grows in your life isn't going to be godliness. It's not that those things are always bad, and it's okay to enjoy them sometimes. But growing into a godly young man who reflects His character to others is a more important investment of your time and energy.

You might be thinking, "I'm just eight! (or nine or ten or twelve). I'm too young to live for Jesus!" Think about this:

- Daniel was a teenager when he stood up to the rulers of Babylon (Daniel 1:8).
- Jeremiah was seventeen when God called him to be a prophet (Jeremiah 1:6).
- David was young when he took on Goliath (1 Samuel 17:12–51).
- Samuel was still a boy when God spoke to him (1 Samuel 3).
- Jesus Himself impressed the religious leaders when He was only twelve (Luke 2:41–47).

If living for God at your age feels impossible, you might be believing a lie:

"I'm too young to _____."

This lie shows up in many different ways to keep boys like you from planting good things in their lives. Sometimes it sounds like one of these lies:

- "I'm too young to read my Bible on my own."
- "I'm too young to pray."
- "I'm too young to serve at church."
- "I'm too young to make a difference."
- "I'm too young to give generously."
- "I'm too young for God to listen to me."

While you may not be able to do everything you want to do yet, there is so much you can do! **You are planting and watering seeds right now that determine the kind of man you will become.**

The apostle Paul once had a friend named Timothy. Even though Timothy was young, Paul trusted him to help start new churches and lead people to Jesus. Timothy may not have had as much experience as someone older, but his life produced remarkable "fruit" that made it clear that he had been planting and watering the right kinds of seeds.

Paul wrote a letter to Timothy, encouraging him to continue to grow in his love for Jesus. That letter is preserved for us in Scripture.

> Don't let anyone think less of you because you are young. Be an example to all believers in what you say, in the way you live, in your love, your faith, and your purity. (1 Timothy 4:12)

Paul's words to young Timothy apply to your life today: don't let anyone look down on you because you're young; set an example for others!

Look at that verse again, and make a list of the kinds of "seeds" Paul encouraged Timothy to keep watering. (Hint: they are the areas in which Paul told Timothy to set an example for others).

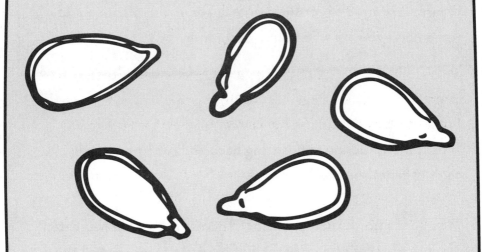

Notice, Paul didn't say, "Set an example with how many free throws you can make," or "Set an example in how many levels of your favorite video game you can beat."

Those pursuits can add a lot of fun and excitement to your life, but they can't help you grow in godliness. Whether you've been following Jesus for a few years or just a few days, if you want to grow to be more like Him, you must take simple steps every day like reading your Bible, praying, asking forgiveness when you've sinned, and loving others well. Those are all things you can do right now! As you continue to pursue becoming more like Him, He will grow something amazing in your life.

If you're reading this book, you're not too young to live for **Jesus!** Don't fall for the lie that what you're doing today doesn't really matter. It does. If you are willing to obey God now, you will be willing to take radical steps of obedience in the future. Take time to consider what seeds you're planting and remember: **you are who you're becoming.**

· · ·

"I'm stuffed," Lenny said, sitting back and rubbing his belly. "I can't eat another bite!"

"You gonna finish that last taco?" Thomas asked. He had eaten his entire basket of nachos, one of his dad's tacos, and all the chips and queso.

"Go for it," Lenny said, pushing his basket toward his brother.

"Where are you putting all of that?" Dad asked.

"I'm planting," Thomas said as he bit into another loaded taco.

"What do you mean, bud?" Dad asked.

"Well, you said we are who we're becoming," Thomas replied. "I figure if I'm becoming a six-foot-eight power forward, I better get to eating! I'm planting the seeds that will grow into an all-star basketball player."

They all had a good laugh about that. After cleaning up their table and leaving a generous tip for their friendly server, Dad, Lenny, and Thomas got back in the van for their final stretch of the journey.

. . .

BONUS LIE:
"It doesn't matter what I watch, read, or listen to."

TRUTH:
Your heart is worth protecting.

Dad watched the gauge on the dash dip closer and closer to empty. He pulled the van under the metal awning of a Texaco station.

"Can we get snacks?" Lenny asked.

"You boys are always hungry!" Dad said with a smile. "Let me finish filling up first."

As Dad pumped the gas and paid at the pump, Thomas cleaned the windshield, a responsibility he'd taken on a couple of years ago even though he had to stand on his tiptoes.

"Squeaky clean," he announced.

"Good work, bud."

Unintentionally, they lined up single file like a train, with Dad as the engine and Lenny as the caboose. They'd just stepped inside the store when Dad stopped in his tracks, did a 180-degree turn and said, "Let's go, boys!"

"But," they started to protest.

"No buts," Dad said. "Turn around and head back to the van."

"What was that about?" Lenny asked as he climbed back into his seat and shut the door.

"Yeah, I really wanted some Skittles," Thomas whined.

"The cost was too high," Dad said.

"How do you know?" Thomas asked. "We didn't even get to check the price!"

"I'm not talking about the cost of the Skittles," Dad said. His tone let the boys know he was serious. "The back wall of that gas station was covered with posters of girls in bikinis."

"What's the big deal, Dad?" Lenny asked. "I've seen girls in swimsuits before."

"What's your most valuable possession?" Dad asked as he put the van in drive.

"Probably my baseball cards," Lenny replied.

"The compass you gave me last year for my birthday," Thomas chimed in. "I keep it in the top drawer of my dresser so I never lose it."

"You've got something more valuable than a thousand compasses or baseball cards," Dad said as they took the on-ramp back onto the highway. "Do you know what it is?"

"I'm too tired for riddles!" Lenny moaned.

"I've got some money in my savings account that Grandma set up last year," Thomas guessed.

"This is worth more than all the money in the bank," Dad said. "It's your heart. Remember the book of Proverbs? We've talked about it a lot on this trip because it's a book full of wisdom that will help you live out God's Truth. Proverbs 4:23 says, 'Guard your heart above all else, for it determines the course of your life.' Your heart is more valuable than anything you can buy or sell and it needs to be protected."

"Someday I hope you marry a woman who loves Jesus and loves you," Dad continued, "but you're not ready for that yet, so whether it's looking at posters in a gas station or pictures online, or listening to music that stirs up certain emotions, or watching movies that make you crave things you shouldn't have, the cost of letting your guard down is just too high. Got it?"

"Got it," Lenny said.

"Got it," Thomas agreed.

It was the kind of conversation they'd need to have again. Guarding the heart is not a one-time thing, but for now they were content to put some miles between themselves and the gas station, knowing the future would bring plenty of opportunities to choose to protect their minds by guarding their hearts.

. . .

As the minutes turned into miles, Thomas's eyelids felt heavy. He slumped sideways in his seat and curled into a ball. Soon enough he was dreaming about feeding Earl a giant plate of nachos. Soon Lenny was snoozing too. As the clock on the dash turned over to midnight, Dad hit the accelerator while both boys enjoyed their last car-trip nap.

"Oh, I can't wait to get home, home, home . . ." Dad repeated this chorus, though he knew no one was listening.

With less than an hour to go, there was no stopping them now.

LIE #10:

"I don't need to tell anyone that I follow Jesus."

TRUTH:

God wants you to "go and tell."

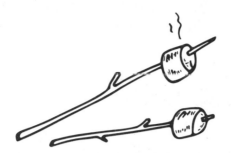

It was a year later and the evening of Lenny's thirteenth birthday. In celebration, they had re-created their epic adventure with a family campout in the backyard.

A fire crackled in front of them. Sister Lucy was covered in sticky marshmallow and smeared chocolate. Mikey looked at his brother with big, round eyes. Lenny was leading the family in a bedtime Bible story, a responsibility he had taken on two or three nights a week for the last several months.

Sure, he was barely a teenager. He wasn't ready to pastor a church or even go to Bible college, but helping others know Jesus and love His Word was his growing passion. He knew that if that was how he hoped to spend his time "someday," he needed to plant those seeds now.

Tonight, Lenny was telling the story that his dad had told him on their big trip out west: that Jesus

207

called a bunch of average fishermen to be His first followers. In asking them to leave their nets, He was inviting them into the grand adventure.

"Jesus said, 'Come, follow me,'" Lenny said, "'and I will show you how to fish for people.'"

At Lenny's request, Lucy cast the invisible line on an invisible fishing pole, and Mikey pretended he'd been caught.

Momma and Dad laughed and beamed with pride as they watched their son tell his siblings about Jesus.

In the past year, Lenny had learned that Dad was right—following Jesus isn't boring. He wanted his little brother and sister, and all his friends and classmates, to know that becoming like Christ was the most exciting thing that had ever happened to him.

For Thomas, the past year had looked different. After they'd returned home from their big trip, he could tell that God had changed him. Thomas no longer found his worth in being a "good boy." It was kind of weird, but when he realized he could never be good enough to earn God's love, he also discovered a lot of freedom. God loved him even though he made mistakes. He didn't have to keep trying to be perfect.

He'd also learned to lean on God when emotions that made him feel out-of-control threatened to take over his heart and mind. It took practice, and he still made mistakes, but he was learning how to live with Spirit-control.

Still . . . at first, he wanted to keep his new commitment to Jesus private. *This is between me and God,* he reasoned. *No one needs to know.* He was worried that his friends wouldn't understand or that they would think he was weird if he started talking about the Bible and Jesus all the time.

Tag, You're It!

In some ways, the disciples had an experience similar to Lenny's and Thomas's. Jesus invited them to follow Him, and for three years they went to new places, saw new faces, and watched Jesus do things they'd never imagined. It wasn't a road trip, but it must have been an adventure!

They watched as Jesus went to the cross to die for their sins (and for yours!). They were among the first to hear the news that He had risen from the dead three days later. They spent time with Him after His resurrection talking about the plans He had for their future.

Matthew 28 records Jesus' last spoken words on earth. He gave His disciples an earth-shaking, life-changing, lie-squashing mission. **Read about it in Matthew 28:18–20 below. Underline what Jesus told His disciples to do.**

> Jesus came and told his disciples, "I have been given all authority in heaven and on earth. Therefore, go and make disciples of all the nations, baptizing them in the name of the Father and the Son and the Holy Spirit. Teach these new disciples to obey all the commands I have given you. And be sure of this: I am with you always, even to the end of the age."

Jesus' words apply to every Christian, including you! He wants you (yes, you!) to go to places where people don't know about Jesus, teach them what it means to follow Him, and point them to His Word. That doesn't mean you have to hop on a plane and fly somewhere far away. There are likely kids at your school, or on your basketball team, or even in your own family who don't know Jesus. You get to tell them!

Many scholars call these verses "the Great Commission" because Jesus has invited us to be on a great mission with Him to share the Good News around the world.

This is how the book of Matthew ends, but it's not how the disciples' stories ended. The book of Acts tells us that they did exactly what Jesus asked them to do—they told everybody about their Savior. They started churches. They traveled as missionaries. They taught others about Jesus' life. God didn't choose them for this mission because they knew all the right things to say and lived perfect lives. He chose them because He loved them and their love for Him motivated them to shout the Good News from the rooftops!

Though your relationship with Jesus is *personal*, and you can talk to Him just like you're talking to a best friend, it isn't *private*. He wants you to tell other people about the things He has done in your life. The Bible gives lots of clues about how to make the dream of this mission come true. **Check out 1 Peter 3:15.**

> If someone asks about your hope as a believer, always be ready to explain it.

Did that verse say that you have to memorize the entire Bible? Nope.
Did it say you have to live a perfect life? Uh-uh.
Did it say you have to be at least thirty years old to make a difference? No.

It says: when people ask you why you have hope, tell them! Hope has a name. His name is Jesus. You can fulfill the mission God has for you simply by sharing what Jesus has done in your life.

You can prepare for your mission right now. **Make a list of all the amazing things God has done for you.** Think of the gifts He's given you, the ways He has helped you turn from lies and run toward Truth, and the ways you see Him making you more like Him. Write down whatever comes to mind on the list below. Then when someone asks why you smile so often, tell them!

What God Has Done for Me

_____

_____

_____

_____

_____

As fireflies danced around them flicking their tiny bulbs off and on, Thomas poked at the backyard campfire with a stick, wrestling with a feeling that had become more and more familiar. He knew God was asking him to step out of his comfort zone.

"Mom and Dad?" he asked, not looking up from the orange coals glowing in the fire pit.

"Do you think I could invite a couple of friends to church?" he asked. "I know Sunday mornings are already busy, but there are some boys in my class that seem to believe lies about who they are and how to spend their time. Marco just wants to play

video games all day. He says it doesn't matter, since he's just a kid. And the other day Austin told me that no one loves him. It made me feel sad. I want him to know that Jesus loves him, you know?"

Mom and Dad looked at each other and smiled. They often prayed together that Thomas would find the courage to live out his faith in Jesus boldly.

"I think we can make that happen," Dad said.

"If you'd like to invite them over for lunch after," Mom added, "we'd be happy to have them. I'm making spaghetti this week."

Lucy was fast asleep in their momma's arms.

"I'm gonna take this sweet girl to bed," Momma announced.

"You're not going to sleep in the tent with us tonight?" Lenny protested.

"Dad said it's dudes only. Guess I will just have to take one for the team and sleep in my big comfy bed instead of in a sleeping bag," she joked.

"Can I sleep outside?" Mikey asked. He'd just turned five and he wanted to do everything his big brothers got to do.

"You betcha," Dad said.

"But Dad snores!" Thomas announced.

"C'mon," Lenny said, unzipping the tent. "Did I ever tell you the story of the time I won the slingshot championship?" he asked his little brother.

Mikey's eyes got wide again. "Tell me! Tell me!"

"Hold up there, partners," Dad said. "I've got one more surprise for the birthday boy."

He pulled a red and white plastic cooler from under his seat. "I had these delivered just for your special day."

As he opened the lid the boys could see what was inside. Laying on a bed of ice were six frosty glass bottles with orange ink across the front.

"Trusties!" Lenny and Thomas shouted at the same time, grabbing up their bottles and popping the caps off of their favorite root beer.

Like all good stories, the perfect end to their perfect night was just the beginning of a lifetime of adventure.

Become a Lie-Fighter!

Just like the characters in this story, you've just completed a looong journey. You've learned so much about who God is, what His Word says, and what it means to live for Him. Before you close this book and go back to doing other stuff, remember what you learned in the very beginning of this book. There are two very real beings who want control over your mind and actions. One tells the Truth; the other is a liar.

Fill in the chart below. Write down the truths you've learned in this book and the lies you've rejected.

Lie	Truth
_____	_____
_____	_____
_____	_____
_____	_____
_____	_____
_____	_____

Satan will never stop lying. It's who he is! And his lies aren't always easy to spot because sometimes they sound a lot like Truth. But you have everything you need to be a lie-fighter! You have:

- Jesus as your Savior
- The Holy Spirit living within you
- God's people to help you when you fall

AND, you have God's Word to show you what is true about God and about you. Remember what Jesus said in John 17:17?

"Your word is truth." (ESV)

The more you know the Truth, the less these lies will work their way into your mind. That means the best way to fight the enemy is to pick up God's Word. Remember what you learned earlier in this book: the Bible is more than a book—it's a sword!

In Ephesians 6:10–13, Paul wrote about how to live free from the lies of the Evil One. The imagery he used was that of a soldier preparing for a fierce battle! He wrote,

A final word: Be strong in the Lord and in his mighty power. Put on all of God's armor so that you will be able to stand firm against all strategies of the devil. For we are not fighting against flesh-and-blood enemies, but against evil rulers and authorities of the unseen world, against mighty powers in this dark world, and against evil spirits in the heavenly places.

Therefore, put on every piece of God's armor so you will be able to resist the enemy in the time of evil. Then after the battle you will still be standing firm.

Paul's words are a reminder that:
1. You are in a battle!
2. God wants you to be strong.
3. He has given you what you need to stand against lies.
4. You *can* stand firm.

Read the rest of Paul's words below. Using words from the passage, fill in each piece of armor with what it's made from.

Stand your ground, putting on the belt of truth and the body armor of God's righteousness. For shoes, put on the peace that comes from the Good News so that you will be fully prepared. In addition to all of these, hold up the shield of faith to stop the fiery arrows of the devil. Put on salvation as your helmet, and take the sword of the Spirit, which is the word of God. (Ephesians 6:14–17)

Picture yourself wearing that gear. You've got the gospel to protect your mind. You've got Jesus' righteousness to protect your heart. You've got a mission to move your feet where they need to go. You've got a shield to deflect flaming darts hurled at you by your enemy. And you have a sword—the Bible—to help you fight against every lie that Satan throws your way.

Without the Bible you are left with no weapon. The Bible teaches you what is true so that you can easily spot lies when they are hurled at you and fight back.

Did you notice what other piece of armor Paul connected to the Truth? (Hint: look back at verse 14.) The belt! Here's another way to say that verse.

> Stand up and do not be moved. Wear a belt of truth around your body. (NLV)

Roman soldiers in Paul's day wore a belt that was a lot different from the leather version you might wear to church. It was a thick, heavy band made of leather and metal, with a big protective piece that hung down in the front of it. The belt held the soldier's sword and other weapons in place.

Your belt of Truth holds everything in place too. It helps you make right choices. It keeps you living in peace. It guards your heart and your mind. You have to put it on to keep the other stuff in place. How? The answer is pretty simple: **think about the Truth every day.**

That might look like getting up early and reading a proverb a day. It might mean finding an audio Bible you like and listening to it each night before bed. It might mean joining a Bible study at school or attending a Sunday school class at church. Maybe you will start a collection of your favorite Bible verses and tape them to your bedroom door. It doesn't matter how you do it, but get into God's Word every single day! Each time you do, you are putting on standard-issue armor for every soldier who wants to win the war against lies.

God has already won the victory. He has given you everything you need to push back against the enemy's lies. You are fully armed with His Truth.

Stand firm!

30-Day Journey through the Book of John

We hope this book inspires you to make reading God's Word a daily habit. If you don't know where to start, consider reading through the book of John like Lenny and Thomas did.

This reading plan will help you read the book of John in thirty days. We left room for you to skip a couple of "Grace Days" each week to rest or just in case you get extra busy. For added adventure, invite your family to read along with you.

☐ **Day 1: Who Is Jesus?**
Text: John 1:1–34

☐ **Day 2: The First Disciples**
Text: John 1:35–51

☐ **Day 3: Shaking Things Up**
Text: John 2, whole chapter

☐ **Day 4: A Meeting in the Dark**
Text: John 3:1–21

☐ **Day 5: Less and Less**
Text: John 3:22–36

☐ **Day 6: Grace Day**

☐ **Day 7: Grace Day**

☐ **Day 8: Living Water**
Text: John 4:1–42

☐ **Day 9: Jesus Heals**
Text: John 4:43–5:15

☐ **Day 10: "I Tell You the Truth"**
Text: John 5:16–47

☐ **Day 11: Leftovers!**
Text: John 6:1–59

☐ **Day 12: The Going Gets Tough**
Text: John 6:60–7:24

☐ **Day 13: Grace Day**

☐ **Day 14: Grace Day**

☐ **Day 15: Living Water**
Text: John 7:25–53

☐ **Day 16: Light of the World**
Text: John 8:1–30

☐ **Day 17: Sent**
Text: John 8:31–59

☐ **Day 18: Look!**
Text: John 9, whole chapter

☐ **Day 19: Shepherds and Sheep**
Text: John 10, whole chapter

☐ **Day 20: Grace Day**

☐ **Day 21: Grace Day**

☐ **Day 22: Wake the Dead**
Text: John 11, whole chapter

☐ **Day 23: Walk in the Light**
Text: John 12:1–36

☐ **Day 24: Dirty Feet**
Text: John 12:37–13:38

☐ **Day 25: The Gift Is Coming!**
Text: John 14, whole chapter

☐ **Day 26: True Vine**
Text: John 15, whole chapter

☐ **Day 27: Time Is Short**
Text: John 16, whole chapter

☐ **Day 28: Jesus Prayed for Y-O-U!**
Text: John 17, whole chapter

☐ **Day 29: Arrested, Beaten, Killed**
Text: John 18–19
Note: These chapters describe the horrible things that Jesus endured so that we could be free from sin. They can be hard to read and understand. Find an adult to read them with you, and then talk through any questions you have.

☐ **Day 30: He's Alive!**
Text: John 20–21

Please & Thank Yous

How many times have you heard your mom say, "What's the magic word?" or your dad say, "Say thank you, son"? Too many times to count? That's because good manners are important, and we want to use ours to say please and thank you to some of the people who made this book possible.

Let's start with the thank yous:

Eli—You are the best son a mom and dad could ever ask for. We are so proud of the young man you are becoming. Thank you for being such a joy to parent.

Noble—You are thoughtful, helpful, diligent, and focused. You are so wonderful. Thank you for the million ways you make our lives better.

Judah—You have been our greatest champion throughout this entire book. We are still smiling about the day you dressed up as a bookshelf at school so that everyone would know your parents are authors. ☺ Your enthusiasm to hear this book as we wrote it kept us motivated. Thank you for being such a remarkable son.

Ezra—You bring sunshine to our family every day. Thank you for making us smile. We look forward to a zillion adventures with you.

Robert and Nancy Wolgemuth—We are inspired by your love for Jesus, God's Word, and for families. Thank you for writing *Lies Women Believe* and *Lies Men Believe*, two powerful books that we leaned on heavily to write this one. Thank you for having faith in us to take what you wrote and shape it for boys to read and for your constant encouragement along the way. When we grow up, we want to be just like you!

Dannah Gresh—Thank you for being our friend, our mentor, and our guide for this and so many other adventures. Your passion to see children know Jesus has had a profound impact on us. You have loved our boys well since before they were born. Your wise and winsome approach to writing *Lies Girls Believe* helped us know what to do. Yours is a lead worth following.

Judy, Amanda, Erik, and the team at Moody—It truly takes a village to write a book, and we have the best village in the world. Thank you specifically to Judy and Amanda for casting vision and making this project into what it is today. We couldn't have done it without you. Thank you, Erik, for your creative direction. You took black and white words and turned them into a book any boy would love to read. Thank you!

Jesus—We saved the best for last. Thank you, Jesus, for Your work in our lives. Without You, we'd be stuck in lies without hope. But You have rescued and redeemed us! You are teaching us to walk in Your truth. Thank You! We will spend the rest of our lives celebrating who You are and all You've done.

Now it's time for a please:

To you, young reader, please take what you've learned in this book and share it with others. Tell your friends, neighbors, and teachers that freedom from lies is possible because Jesus is the Truth! Thank you for taking this journey with us. We love you!